HOW [NOT] TO GROW

40 COMMON MISTAKES TO AVOID WHEN WRITING LYRICS FOR YOUR SONGS

BRIAN OLIVER

Published by Big **6** Publishing
www.thehitformula.com

COPYRIGHT © 2016 by Brian Oliver
The moral right of the author has been asserted.
All rights reserved.

No part of this publication may be reproduced, stored in or introduced into a retrieval system, or transmitted, in any form or by any means, electronic, mechanical, photocopying, recording or otherwise, without the prior permission in writing of the copyright owner, except in the case of brief excerpts or quotations embodied in published articles and reviews. Nor shall this publication be otherwise circulated in any form of binding or cover other than that in which it is published and without a similar condition, including this condition, being imposed on the subsequent purchaser.

Limit of Liability/Disclaimer of Warranty

The publisher and the author make no representations or warranties with respect to the accuracy or completeness of the contents of this work and specifically disclaim all warranties, including without limitation warranties of fitness for a particular purpose. No warranty may be created or extended by sales or promotional materials. The advice and strategies contained herein may not be suitable for every situation. This work is sold with the understanding that the publisher and the author are not engaged in rendering legal, accounting or other professional services. If professional assistance is required, the services of a competent professional person should be sought. Neither the publisher nor the author shall be liable for damages arising herefrom.

Published by Big **6** Publishing
www.thehitformula.com

ISBN-13: 978-1537097787
ISBN-10: 1537097784

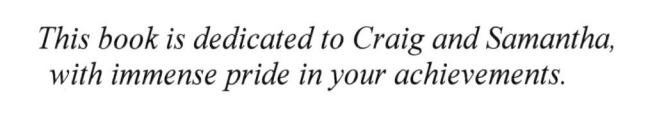

This book is dedicated to Craig and Samantha, with immense pride in your achievements.

ABOUT THE AUTHOR

Brian Oliver is a highly experienced music publisher, songwriter, musician and music consultant who has been involved in the music industry for over 25 years.

As a publisher, he has worked on the songs of legendary writers such as Neil Diamond, Janis Ian, Albert Hammond, Chip Taylor, Gilbert O'Sullivan and John & Johanna Hall, as well as bands like The Stranglers, Spandau Ballet and The Shadows, and leading film & TV composer Colin Towns. He has also been a consultant to major companies such as Universal Music, Warner Music and BMG.

He is the author of the five-star rated book, *How [Not] to Write a Hit Song! 101 Common Mistakes to Avoid If You Want Songwriting Success*. This much-praised book takes a close look at the essential elements consistently found in the structure, melodies and lyrics of all hit songs. It highlights the most common errors made when these key components are built into a song—so that new songwriters can try to avoid such mistakes in their own songs.

# # # #

TABLE OF CONTENTS

INTRODUCTION..3
#1 Thinking Lyrics Are Just Like Poems...............7
#2 Not Listening To What The Melody Is Saying....11
#3 Getting Lost In Time....................................15
#4 Making Your Lyrics Too Complex................ 19
#5 Failing To Make An Emotional Connection...... 24
#6 Writing For Yourself Not The Listener........... 29
#7 Writing Happy Love Songs........................ 33
#8 A Title Nobody Can Remember................... 38
#9 Not Writing From The Title......................... 42
#10 Putting Your Title In The Wrong Place......... 45
#11 Not Highlighting Important Phrases............. 47
#12 Trying To Force Your Lyrics......................51
#13 Not Taking Steps To Avoid Writer's Block.... 55
#14 Trying To Say Too Much..........................61
#15 Playing It Too Safe.................................64
#16 Weak Characterization.............................69
#17 Not Making Sense Of Your Senses...............74
#18 Telling Not Showing................................81
#19 Unconvincing Choice Of Verbs...................86
#20 Where's The Detail?................................89

#21 Not Keeping Your Imagery Simple…………...93
#22 Saying The Same Old Thing…………………95
#23 Too Many Clichés……………………………100
#24 Not Tapping Listeners On The Shoulder…….103
#25 Failing To Support The Song Form…………106
#26 A Lyrical Hook That Doesn't Stick…………108
#27 Not Using The Bridge………………………111
#28 Too Little Repetition (Or Too Much)………113
#29 Inconsistent Viewpoint………………………115
#30 Losing Your Balance…………………………118
#31 Too Many Words……………………………121
#32 Not Enough Contrast………………….....…123
#33 Not Enough Metric Variation……………….126
#34 Inconsistent Use Of Tense……………….....132
#35 Not Letting The Lyric Move Forward………136
#36 Your Rhymes Are Too Predictable………….140
#37 Not Varying Your Rhyme Patterns………….145
#38 Not Checking Singability……………………149
#39 Not Using Enough Polish……………………155
#40 The Lyrics Aren't Clear On Your Demo…….160
CHECKLIST…………………………………….163
Other books by Brian Oliver……………………177

# # # #

INTRODUCTION

"It's important to learn from your mistakes, but it is better to learn from other people's mistakes..."
—Jim Rohn

EVERY WRITER has his or her own unique approach to the creative process. But, in my experience as a music publisher, there are certain mistakes that are common to all weak lyrics.

The purpose of this book, therefore, is to help you hone your skills and improve your lyrical craft by highlighting the most common lyric writing mistakes that I've observed, so you can try to avoid them in your own songs.

There are many excellent publications out there that can teach you the theory of lyric writing and song structure in academic detail. But my own belief is that too much emphasis on theory can weaken the inventiveness that comes naturally and spontaneously to many writers.

Instead of simply allowing ideas to flow freely and instinctively, an aspiring writer's creativity can end up being constrained by the perceived need to follow the theoretical 'rules' they've been given.

That's why this is more of a 'How Not To' book rather than just another 'How To' book on writing lyrics. It looks at the key components that are consistently found in the structure of hit song lyrics, and shows how to avoid the errors that are commonly made when these various elements are built into a lyric.

And you don't need any knowledge of songwriting theory to be able to follow this book. The content is presented in a non-technical way that is designed to make it easy and quick to digest.

As I've said to many developing writers I've worked with over the years, when you start a writing session just write what comes into your head. Don't keep stopping to check whether each word, phrase, rhyme or line length adheres to the 'rules'. Just let the words flow from your imagination and onto the page.

When you've finished, that's the time to go back and check what you've written.

With each new lyric you write, you can use the tips and checklist in this book to make sure you haven't fallen into any of the traps that new writers sometimes fall into.

When a new idea suddenly hits you—and all the pieces drop into place so quickly that the lyric almost writes itself—it's very easy to fall into the trap of rushing straight into a studio and recording a demo. You then confidently submit the song to a music publisher or record company believing it's the best thing you've ever written—only to suffer the agony of having the song rejected and returned.

Sometimes it's best just to slow down, take a step back, and re-examine each element of your new song.

If you don't spend a little more time polishing your lyrics, there is a danger that they may still contain some weaknesses that you failed to spot first time around.

Because competition is intense and music industry standards are now set very high, even professional writers know that every new song they create will probably need several re-writes before they have the final version. They've learned that creating a great lyric usually requires 10% writing and 90% re-writing.

So it's more important than ever to avoid the pitfalls that other new writers fall into and make sure your songs are the best, and stand out from the crowd.

That's why one of the purposes of this book is, in effect, to give you a benchmark that you can measure your own lyrics against, no matter how 'finished' you think they are. The aim is to help you develop your own unique lyric writing style while avoiding fundamental mistakes at each key stage in the song development process.

I hope this book will help to guide you and your lyrics on the road to success. And, to paraphrase baseball legend Yogi Berra, who was known for his wise Yogi-isms: "Try not to make too many wrong mistakes". Use the tips and checklist in this book to avoid them …

Good luck!

Brian Oliver, August 2016

#1
THINKING LYRICS ARE JUST LIKE POEMS

"Lyrics have elements that could be shared with poetry. But they're not poems ... They're meant to be sung. They come out of the rhythm of the music, as opposed to creating your own rhythm of the words"
—Paul Simon

TO WRITE effective song lyrics, it is important to recognize from the outset that poetry and lyrics are not the same.

You may be great at creating beautiful poetry, but when it comes to writing song lyrics you have to employ a completely different set of skills. The type of language, rhyme and descriptive imagery used impressively in a poem can often end up sounding pretentious when applied to a song.

As award-winning lyricist Stephen Sondheim puts it: "Lyrics have to be underwritten. That's why poets generally make poor lyric writers because the language is too rich. You get drowned in it."

Of course, good poetry and great lyrics do share the same ability to reach people on an emotional level. As the legendary lyricist Sammy Cahn once remarked: "A poem is meant for the eye while a lyric is meant for the ear, but both reach the mind and touch the heart."

A poem and a lyric can both create powerful imagery through the potent use of devices such as metaphor, simile and personification. Some lyricists—notably in the hip-hop genre—can be remarkably poetic. And poetry can sometimes be musical in the way certain words and phrases play off each other. But they aren't the same thing.

Poetry is created to stand alone and connect with people by being read on the page; a lyric is delivered to the ear and is intended to be sung and heard in conjunction with music. Lyric writing is therefore the art of shaping words for music (or to music) and requires an astute combination of phonetics, grammar, semantics, linguistics, metrics, rhyme and rhythm.

As Elton John's long-time lyricist Bernie Taupin has said: "My lyrics are nothing like poetry. They're supposed to be heard with a melody. I don't like people taking my lyrics out of context and reading them as poetry, because they were written to be sung. They were not written to be recited."

Lyricists also have to work their magic under much tighter constraints than poets. "Lyrics are an unforgivingly compact form", Stephen Sondheim wrote in his book *Finishing the Hat*.

As a poet you can pour out your feelings on page after page of dense and structurally complex text. As a lyricist, though, every single word counts. You only have a limited amount of space in which to work. For a pop single lasting less than four minutes, the space available is typically 15-20 lines (excluding repeated choruses).

This means you have to be more concise than a poet. You have to use as few words as possible ... yet still set the scene, express yourself clearly, and evoke a feeling in the listener. As Neil Diamond once observed: "Songs are life in 80 words or less".

When people are listening to a song, the music moves forward quickly so they don't have time to dwell on a particular word or line. Unlike poetry—which is usually read at a much slower pace—listeners can't go back and re-read a lyric line to see what the words actually mean.

"If you're writing a song, you have to write something that can be understood serially," explained English poet James Fenton who is also a former Professor of Poetry at Oxford University.

"When you're reading a poem that's written for the page," he said, "your eye can skip up and down. You can see the thing whole. But you're not going to see the thing whole in a song. You're going to hear it in series, and you can't skip back."

That's why the majority of hit songs today contain lyrical images and descriptive phrases that are easily understood and can connect with the listener's ears immediately.

Lyrical language also has to be much simpler than poetry and you have to get to the point quickly whilst, at the same time, striving to create strong images using everyday words. A poet can focus on the creative use of free-flowing language, and most poems—whether they're fixed form, blank verse, or free verse—tend to be linear journeys that move from idea to idea, and line to line, without any repetition.

A good lyricist, however, has to learn how to use important structural tools of songwriting such as the frequent repetition of key words and lyrical lines.

Repetition is a device that is vital to many of today's hit songs (especially in choruses and in the title line over a song's melodic hook).

Unlike a poet, therefore, when you're developing your lyrical idea you have to take account of the repeated sections—and try to deepen the meaning of those sections each time the listener hears them.

To achieve this, the lyrics in the unrepeated lines (usually in the verse) must move the story forward, while the repeated sections have to hammer the song home so that listeners will remember it.

A lyricist also has to work within the confines of a clearly defined melodic structure and rhythm.

This requires a good understanding of how verses, pre-choruses, choruses and bridges work together to hold the listener's interest.

The best way to develop this skill is to dissect and analyze some of your favorite writers' songs and see how their lyrics and rhyming patterns work within each song.

This will help you to identify the lyrical building blocks used in a successful song structure and see how the different sections are joined together.

Then try writing your own lyrics based on these proven templates.

"Just because something looks good on the page doesn't guarantee it can be a viable lyric," observed Michael Chabon, the acclaimed American author whose lyrics feature on more than half the tracks on Mark Ronson's chart-topping album *Uptown Special*.

He said the experience had shown him the difference between writing lyrics and prose.

"Sometimes you need a line not to be brilliant or memorable or dazzling," he said. "You just need it to fit …".

# # # #

#2

NOT LISTENING TO WHAT THE MELODY IS SAYING

*"The right words and notes in the right places …
That's what makes the difference between
a good song and a great song."*
—Prince

WRITING LYRICS that don't match the emotion, mental images and harmonic colors contained in a song's musical soundbed is a common mistake made by many new lyricists.

They don't realize that it's essential to make sure their words and the melody belong together.

Many developing writers think this means simply making sure their words fit naturally into the melody.

However, it's not enough just to sit down and write some words that match the meter and rhythm of the tune.

Aligning stressed syllables or key words with downbeats or accented notes can, of course, play a powerful role in conveying meaning—but your lyrics must first be built on the mood and emotional foundations laid down by the melody and the chord progression.

The great George Gershwin once described songwriting as "an emotional science", and scientific studies have shown that a wide range of notes can imply joy or uneasiness, while a narrower range of notes can suggest tranquility, sadness or triumph. Major chords often convey happiness or joy, while minor chords are associated with sadness.

Using a mix of minor chords and major chords can add extra depth and color to a song. And surprising listeners with an unexpected chord change can produce a moment of tension before the music eventually resolves. It is this tension and release in the music that can stimulate a strong emotional response within the listener (including the release of dopamine, our brain's 'feel good' chemical).

Despite these 'scientific' manipulations of the melody, a large part of the emotional power of a song still lies in what the words mean for each listener personally. That's why it's important for your lyrics to not only encapsulate the melody but also tell a story that people can relate to—something that reminds them of a place, an event or a person in their life.

It's the ability to combine music and lyrics to make listeners feel—to release that dopamine—that keeps them coming back for more.

So, whether you're a lyricist working with a composer, or a topliner who writes lyrics over someone else's track, it's essential to study the structure of the melody and listen to what the melody and chord progression are trying to say before you get to work on the words. Close your eyes and see what kind of images are being created in your head by the music.

The legendary lyricist Hal David always gave this advice to new writers: "The first step is to listen to the music very closely, not so much to learn what the notes are, but to see what the music is saying to you."

"If you're a lyric writer, you should hear the music talking to you," he said. "I'd often write dummy lyrics to help me retain the melody, particularly if the melody is a little complex."

At the other end of the musical spectrum, US rock singer-songwriter Beck once described how he creates his famously oblique and ironic lyrics: "Usually, the music inspires the lyrics. The lyrics just sort of fall off like a bunch of crumbs from the melody."

If it's your own melody, some lyric lines may come instinctively as the chords and tune evolve. But instead of trying to structure a complete, perfect lyric, simply start by humming vowel sounds that fit your melody ... and think about the kind of rhyme treatment that would work best with the melodic phrasing.

When Stevie Wonder was asked to describe his approach to writing lyrics, he said: "A lot of times when I start a song, all I have is a melody or a basic idea for a lyric. I'll use vowel sounds in place of lyrics. Then I'll make the lyrics fit the inflection of the sound."

Try recording a simple instrumental demo of your melody (or listen to the composer's demo or the beatmaker's basic track) and make a note of how you feel as the melody and chords progress. For example, is there a lift in the chorus from minor to major chords?

Make a list of the words and phrases that jump out at you from the music. Use a thesaurus to find the most descriptive and sensory words that capture what you're experiencing and add them to your word list as well.

Then put the list aside for a few days …

When you come back to your list with fresh eyes, pick out the words or phrases that really jump out and look like they could be combined to tell a story that reflects the melody—then use them as the basis of your lyric for the song.

When describing her highly distinctive approach to songwriting, Sia Furler explained: "The melody comes first and then I'll choose lyrical content from a list of concepts I have in my phone, and whenever I think of one I write it down. So I'll just scroll through all of my notes and look for concepts that feel like the melody."

As Ray Stevens, the Grammy-winning US country singer-songwriter, once remarked: "The human brain is a funny thing; it's very susceptible to tempo and melody. If you put the right words to it, it becomes very influential."

# # # #

#3
GETTING LOST IN TIME

"It's so important to know what's happening around you with records, radio, TV, everything. You've got to keep abreast of what's going on to stay on top of it all."
—Lamont Dozier

SONGWRITING IS a living thing. It continues to develop with each new generation of artists and music.

At the same time, language is continually evolving too, with new words that have entered common usage being added to dictionaries almost every month. So it's vital to make sure you are creating lyrics that sound current and will appeal to today's audiences.

Don't make the mistake of using phrases that could have been written decades ago. Some of them may have sounded clever and 'cool' back then, but they could come across as old-fashioned, dated or twee today.

If your lyrics don't sound like they belong on today's radio stations, music TV channels, or streaming services, you'll never be able to achieve any success with them.

Remember, you're competing with today's top professional writers. That's why it's important to be sensitive to trends and keep your lyrics up-to-date. Don't get caught in a time warp ...

Since the 1990s, hip hop has had a significant impact on the structure and content of pop lyrics, especially dance-oriented pop and electronic dance music. Lyrics are an essential part of hip hop culture and their influence has resulted in greater diversity in terms of vocabulary and song topics. Hip hop has also contributed to a heavier emphasis on the repetition of vowel sounds to create elaborate internal rhyming within lyrics (assonance), and the repetition of the same sounds in stressed syllables of a phrase (alliteration).

In the lyrics of the new wave of singer-songwriters—Ed Sheeran, for example—you can hear the influences of rappers like Eminem and Jay-Z blending with the introspective balladry and philosophical lyrics and metaphors of 1970s troubadours such as Joni Mitchell, Carole King and James Taylor.

When asked about the increasing blurring of boundaries between music genres, Ed Sheeran told the *Daily Telegraph*: "If you keep your musical horizons wide then you expect different shades to come through. It's like mixing two worlds and getting the best of both."

A number of studies have looked at how the lyrics of chart hits have changed over the years. These analyses have generally found that today's songs are still predominantly about love and romance, but in recent decades popular subject matter has shifted from slushy and sentimental lyrics to a greater emphasis on sex and much darker and angrier themes.

The language used in some of today's lyrics has become more explicit, especially in contemporary R&B songs that have sexual undertones.

One study—by data artist and researcher Nickolay Lamm—found that words like 'money', 'body', 'foul', 'hate' and 'kill' now tend to pop up more often in lyrics than they used to, while the words 'lonely', 'sad', 'heart' and 'I love you' were more common in the past.

Whereas songwriters in the 1960s tended to use a lot of poetic vocabulary about love, escape, loneliness and loss, researchers found that topics such as sex, freedom, work and suicide became more common in the 1970s. Meanwhile, analyses of chart hits in the 1980s show that lust was the most common topic for lyrics in this decade (followed by love, nostalgia, unity, partying and dancing). These same themes also spilled over into the 1990s, 2000s and 2010s, along with messages about freedom, money and empowerment.

"In earlier lyrics, love was easy and positive, and about two people," said researcher Jean M. Twenge, a professor of Psychology at San Diego State University. "Recent songs are about what the individual wants, and how she or he has been disappointed or wronged."

However, a study conducted in 2014 by David Taylor of the data science blog Prooffreader.com, found that lyrics in the 2010s tended to be more inclusive than in the past (with greater use of the word 'we' compared with the 'you', 'ya' and 'u' of the 1990s and 2000s).

When it comes to your own lyrics, the best way to make sure they sound fresh and modern is to study what today's hit songwriters are doing. Analyze current trends by listening to what's being played on the radio and on music streaming services.

Instead of buying the sheet music or grabbing lyrics from online sources, dissect your favorite songs by taking the lyrics down yourself by ear.

This exercise will help you to identify and absorb the words, phrases, line lengths, rhyming patterns and types of rhymes being used by today's top writers. Figuring out the lyrics by yourself in this way will give you a much better understanding of the building blocks used to create hit lyrics. It'll show you how the different sections of a song are joined together lyrically—and you'll find there are standard forms around which most lyrics are organized today.

Then try writing your own lyrics based on these proven templates … adding something original of your own, of course, to make your song stand out from the crowd.

####

#4
MAKING YOUR LYRICS TOO COMPLEX

"I used to think hits were based on intellect. But clever doesn't sell, intellect doesn't sell. Emotional content sells ... It's when listeners go, 'Yeah, I know. I feel that too'."
—Paul Williams

ASPIRING LYRICISTS often make the mistake of trying too hard to impress music publishers and A&R reps (and sometimes even their songwriting collaborators) by coming up with lyrics stuffed with overly complex words and phrases. They don't realize that listeners are likely to be turned off if they hear convoluted phrases that don't make sense to them.

A great lyric doesn't have to be technically intricate. It just needs to be able to reach out and touch people—and arouse their interest—without listeners having to struggle to grasp what it is you're trying to communicate to them.

As the great lyricist Stephen Sondheim once remarked: "Music blows lyrics up very quickly, and suddenly they become more than art. They become pompous and they become self-conscious ... I firmly believe that lyrics have to breathe and give the audience's ear a chance to understand what's going on."

If your lyrics are too complicated, the song could just end up sounding clumsy. That's why it is important to recognize that there's a big difference between complex words and complex lyrics. Sometimes a lyric can be enjoyably complex, with a deep meaning, but still keep people listening because it is put together in an entertaining way using uncomplicated, everyday language that everyone can understand.

For example, The Beach Boys' 1966 album *Pet Sounds* is regarded as one of the most influential 'art rock' albums of all time. It includes highly complex, introspective songs such as 'You Still Believe in Me' (about faithfulness) and 'I Just Wasn't Made for These Times' (about social alienation). But if you listen to Tony Asher's lyrics, they're really quite simple. 'Don't Talk (Put Your Head on My Shoulder)', for example, opens with the lines: "I can hear so much in your sighs/And I can see so much in your eyes". It's the way Asher's conversational words interact with Brian Wilson's incredible melodies that creates the emotional intensity.

Tony Asher also wrote the lyrics for another *Pet Sounds* track, 'God Only Knows', which is now regarded as one of the greatest songs ever written. It's Paul McCartney's favorite song. But it only has eight lines of lyrics (excluding the repeated title line).

As Asher himself once remarked: "There's something about its simplicity, its naiveté, maybe, that people respond to … The simplicity makes it very personal and tender."

In other words, the lyricist's skill is in telling compelling stories and making an emotional connection with listeners while using familiar, ordinary words in a way that someone might use them in a casual conversation.

So don't fall into the trap of believing that you have to make every line clever or tricky in order to demonstrate your talent and originality.

Using common words in short sentences or fragments of sentences can make your lyrics much easier to follow in real time.

And don't be afraid to repeat key words or phrases throughout your lyric in order to emphasize important ideas. This will make it easier for listeners to comprehend what you're saying without needing further explanation.

Experienced writers know that sounding conversational is an important factor in making a song believable. As The Eagles' Don Henley once explained: "I try to write conversationally ... I try to write like people speak and put the emphasis on the right syllable."

If you analyze the work of some of the world's finest lyricists, you'll find that they tend to create vivid emotional descriptions while using simple, everyday words that the average listener can relate to (including contractions that simulate ordinary speech). They often leave out unimportant words such as 'that'. Hal David, for example, was a master at conveying what he wanted to say in the simplest way possible, despite the complexity of some of Burt Bacharach's melodies.

Great lyricists also enrich commonplace words with a variety of figurative poetic devices such as:

—**Metaphors**: comparing or portraying a person, action, feeling, place or thing as being something else.

—**Similes**: making a direct comparison to show similarities between two different things, usually with the help of the words 'like' or 'as'.

—**Personification**: attributing human characteristics to something non-human (for example: "The waves danced in the moonlight").

Metaphors in particular can be found in common expressions and unassuming words that we hear every day without even noticing them—from ordinary conversations in a café to advertising and news reports on radio and TV.

Elvis Presley's classic 1957 hit, 'All Shook Up' (written by Otis Blackwell), is a good example of how ordinary, everyday words can be used in a metaphor to describe something abstract, such as ideas, feelings, thoughts and emotions.

The song includes the lines: "Her lips are like a volcano that's hot" and "I'm proud to say that she's my buttercup". These metaphors show the listener that the girl's lips are not lips but volcanoes, and she isn't a girl, she's a buttercup.

Allusion is another device that enables lyricists to simplify complex ideas and emotions. An allusion is an indirect reference to a person, place, thing or idea of historical, cultural, literary or political significance.

Allusion saves on word count by not describing in detail the person or thing it refers to.

It's just a passing comment that relies on the listener possessing enough knowledge to spot the allusion and grasp its importance (for example: "He was a natural-born Romeo").

Billy Joel's 1989 Song, 'We Didn't Start the Fire', is famous for containing over 115 allusions to different historical events. It includes lines such as: "Birth control, Ho Chi Minh, Richard Nixon back again/Moonshot, Woodstock, Watergate, punk rock...".

Combining simple and straightforward contemporary words with clever poetic tools—such metaphors, similes, personification and allusion—can give the appearance that an interesting lyric is much more intricate than it really is.

# # # #

#5

FAILING TO MAKE AN EMOTIONAL CONNECTION

"For me to feel confident with one of my songs, it has to really move me. That's how I know I've written a good song ... it's when I start crying. It's when I break out in tears in the vocal booth or in the studio and I'll need a moment to myself."
—Adele

WHETHER YOU'RE purely a lyricist working with a composer ... or a singer-songwriter or a band member who writes both the words and music for your own songs ... or a topliner who writes melodies and lyrics over someone else's soundbeds, it's important to recognize that a song will only become a truly great song if it is able to reach out and touch listeners.

That's why your lyrics must be able to stimulate an emotional response within the people who hear them.

"An editorial in rhyme is not a song," the legendary American folk singer Pete Seeger once remarked. "A good song makes you laugh, it makes you cry, it makes you think."

If you can talk to someone's emotions—and make an impression on them—your song will stick around in their memory.

As the American poet Maya Angelou put it: "People will forget what you said; people will forget what you did; but people will never forget how you made them feel."

Unlike almost any other art form, songs have a unique ability to evoke and express a wide range of emotions.

By skillfully blending melodies, chord progressions, tempo and lyrics, songwriters can convey any kind of feeling—from sadness and the pain of a lost love ... to joy, a sense of overcoming something, or a life-affirming feeling that everything is going to be okay with the world.

Your role as a lyricist is to form a connection with the listener through a skillful choice of words that will clearly communicate a specific message.

The language you use has to evoke an intentional emotion or image in the listener's head and consequently reward them with a moving experience every time they hear your song.

"I search for believability, simplicity and emotional impact," said lyricist Hal David. "Above all, I try to create an emotion to which others can respond."

When a song is capable of making a powerful emotional connection with listeners in this way, the feeling it stimulates within them can continue to have the same effect on subsequent generations too.

Think of how listeners today are still moved by vintage songs such as Irving Berlin's ballad of love and longing, 'What'll I Do?' from 1924; George and Ira Gershwin's 'Someone To Watch Over Me' (1926), Mack Gordon and Harry Warren's 'At Last' (1941), and Cole Porter's 'Ev'ry Time We Say Goodbye' (1944). In the same way, Adele's heart-rending 'Someone Like You' (2011) will probably still have audiences in tears in 2111.

The Bee Gees' Robin Gibb always believed that emotion should be the bedrock of any song. "Putting melody and emotion together can create something magical," he said. "There is something very appealing to all ages when you are singing about human emotions. Songs about human relationships and the human condition will always be the mainstay of popular music because emotions reach out over the decades."

Elton John takes a similar view: "If you write great songs with meaning and emotion, they will last forever."

Music publishers and record labels' A&R reps always want to hear inventive lyrics that avoid clichés and convey an interesting story or message in an easily understandable way.

But they also want words with meaning and emotion that underpin the title and the hook.

This is also true if you're trying to get another artist to cut your songs. You need to be able to offer them an interesting storyline about situations, struggles and hardships that the artist can relate to, and which the artist can then use to evoke an emotional response within his or her fans.

As a writer, you have to take listeners on a memorable and emotional journey. With the help of carefully chosen words and phrases, you have to describe an experience in such a way that listeners can be drawn into the experience ... and then take those emotions with them after the song has finished.

As American singer, songwriter and producer Ryan Tedder says: "Put humanity in a song and people react to that."

In her powerful song 'The Lonely', Christina Perri doesn't just tell us she's feeling lonely. Instead, her opening line shows it's two o'clock in the morning and "the silent sound of loneliness wants to follow me to bed ...".

Leon Huff—one half of the legendary Gamble & Huff songwriting and production team—also believes that a great song has to make you feel a certain way. "Songs have to do something, that's when you get a reaction," he said. "There are some songs on the radio that just play and you don't even know they're there. You hear others and immediately turn it up. There's something to that. It's got to capture your ears, because that's where it hits you first. Then it's got to soothe your soul."

If your lyrics don't come across as genuine and sincere, listeners may find it hard to connect with your song.

Using words found in everyday language can help to create a connection. One way to achieve this is to write as if you're having a personal conversation with the listener, or with a lover or some other person.

"Just talking to somebody that ain't there" is how Bob Dylan described this approach.

Ed Sheeran, for example, says he often uses his lyrics as a form of letting off steam. "It's like when you're angry with someone and you write an email or a letter to that person, and you write everything down but you never give it to them.

He added: "Songwriting is my way of getting out anger, aggression, happiness and love."

Ultimately, therefore, a song lyric is only likely to be successful if it connects to the listener on an emotional level.

Like Adele, if you're moved emotionally by your lyrics, then your song may also connect with other people, and that's what you need to achieve.

Try testing your lyrics on the people closest to you—someone who will give you an honest opinion. If your words don't genuinely move them, your lyrics have failed.

But if you've managed to pull them into your song's world for a few minutes, then that's a good sign of lyric writing success.

###

#6

WRITING FOR YOURSELF NOT THE LISTENER

"You're creating an intimacy that everybody feels, that it's their experience, not yours. I'll never introduce a song and say, now this song is about 'my' broken heart ..."
—Diana Krall

MANY DEVELOPING songwriters make the mistake of writing purely for themselves instead of writing lyrics with the listener in mind. They limit the commercial potential of their songs by only writing about *their* life and *their* world.

If your aim is to earn a living as a writer, your songs need to have broad commercial appeal—which is all that music publishers, record producers and A&R reps are interested in anyway. You have to be careful not to limit your chances by making your lyrics too narrow and too personal.

By all means express yourself by writing passionately about something you're familiar with and believe in, but don't be too insular. Unless you're simply writing to please yourself, or to entertain your family, you're unlikely to achieve substantial success by writing self-centered and self-indulgent lyrics that don't engage listeners.

"Sometimes personal lyrics can be endearing and cool, and make you feel close to the writer," says singer-songwriter Chris Cornell—former frontman with Soundgarden and Audioslave. "But, a lot of times, you get this feeling of 'Why do I care?'"

So don't be like the boring person at a party who only ever wants to talk about himself or herself. People don't want to hear about your problems. They might, however, want to listen if your songs are about experiences, hardships and situations that everyone can relate to—such as a broken love affair, a personal tragedy, or a song about concern for the environment.

As US singer-songwriter Jackson Browne once remarked: "I'm not looking to describe something that's only true of my own circumstances. It's all about reaching inside to something that you have in common with many."

In order to attract listeners' attention and pull them into your song as quickly as possible, you first have to put yourself in their shoes. If you have a good understanding of how you want listeners to feel when they hear your lyrics, it will enable you to develop the song in such a way that people can immediately connect with it and believe the story you're telling is *their* story.

"It means you can sing your song to 85,000 people and they'll sing it back to you for 85,000 different reasons," says Foo Fighters' Dave Grohl.

Giving listeners an impression of something that gets them to fill in details from their own life is a highly effective lyrical device.

If your lyrics can remind someone of a place, an event, or a person in their life then you've got them hooked.

In other words, you have to make them see and *feel* the story—and be part of it—not just hear it.

But it requires carefully-chosen words and phrases that describe an experience so compellingly that every listener can place herself or himself in the story without even thinking about it, and then retain those feelings long after the song has ended.

American singer-songwriter Meghan Trainor has admitted that's she's so concerned about making her songs as relevant as possible to everyone that she deliberately avoids using gendered pronouns or even words like 'you' and 'me'.

"When I write songs, I'll pick a topic but I don't get too specific," she says. "I don't say 'he' or 'she'. I don't say 'you' or 'me.' I avoid all that stuff so I can relate to everyone."

Familiarity is another important device for pulling listeners into the imaginary world of your song. A hint of familiarity will help people to interact with your lyrics.

If you use common, everyday words to describe an emotional situation that reminds people of something that has happened to them in the past—or could happen to them at some point in the future—then this familiarity can make the song feel real.

Top lyricists also get listeners involved in a story by using vivid descriptions of physical senses such as sight, sound, smell, touch and taste.

Once listeners take in all of these images and sensations, they're already in the scene. They can see, hear and touch what's going on. They can feel what the character is feeling. It's their story ...

That's why it is so important to make sure your lyrics are honest, believable and heartfelt, so that everyone can easily relate to them. If your words don't come across as genuine, listeners may find it hard to connect with your song — and they'll easily forget it.

Grammy-nominated English singer-songwriter James Bay shares this view. "Just be honest," he urges. "Tell the truth ... I think that's one of the tricks to lyrics."

As US singer-songwriter Pink once said: "Honest songs can often resonate strongly with listeners who are able to relate to those same experiences, hardships and situations in their own lives—whether it's a broken love affair, a personal tragedy, or family problems."

British songwriter Carla Marie Williams—who wrote hit songs such as 'Runnin'' and 'Freedom' for Beyoncé—believes in "writing from the soul and singing from the heart". Her song 'Runnin'' was written from her own personal experience. "But when Beyoncé and Naughty Boy heard it," she said, "they both related to it. That's the beauty with writing ... people relate."

# # # #

#7

WRITING HAPPY LOVE SONGS

"All good love songs are sad."
—Paul McCartney

IF YOU want to write a great love song, write a sad one. That's the view of many experienced songwriters, including Paul McCartney whose enduring love songs 'Yesterday', 'Let It Be' and 'The Long and Winding Road' overwhelmingly prove this point.

While good feelings inevitably fade, painful ones can stay with us forever—which may be why negative songs about sadness or regret have always had the greatest power to make an emotional connection with people.

In 2015, British singer-songwriter Adele admitted that sadness is the inspiration behind many of her most successful songs. She told NBC's *The Today Show*: "I think [songwriting] is just a way of channeling it. I don't think that sadness is always devastating. It can be quite uplifting and joyful as well. I think you have to let yourself be sad in order to move forward."

Neuroimaging studies have shown that music can activate the parts of the human brain that are typically associated with emotion. As a result, lyrics have the ability to connect with listeners by evoking a wide range of feelings that everyone can relate to—such as love, sadness, joy, anger, happiness, regret, guilt, shame, desire, tranquility, envy and jealousy.

These common human emotions are not just things that happen to us; they are vital components of how we reason and live our lives, and how we think about the past and the future.

This puts a powerful weapon into the hands of the lyricist.

Songs based on potent emotional themes can stimulate a memory in the listener that will cause him or her to reflect on a past event. If your lyrics can make the audience feel the emotion attached to that memory—whether the experience was bitter or sweet, joyful or painful—you've probably got them hooked.

Music's ability to trigger memories or rekindle emotions may be one reason why sad songs about lost love, unrequited love and jealous love have appealed to audiences ever since the dawn of the 'modern' popular love song in the mid-19th century.

These are feelings that most people have experienced at one time in their lives—and well-crafted lyrics can touch listeners by causing them to re-live those emotions.

Take 'After The Ball', the first million-selling 'pop' love song. Written in 1891 by Charles K. Harris, this poignant song tells the story of a man who saw his sweetheart kissing another man at a ball, and refused to listen to her explanation. Many years later, after the woman had died, he discovered that the man was her brother.

"Love is the greatest emotion of all," said Lamont Dozier in an interview with *American Songwriter* magazine. As a member of the legendary songwriting and production team of Holland–Dozier–Holland, he was responsible for Motown classics such as 'Where Did Our Love Go', 'Standing in the Shadows of Love', 'It's the Same Old Song' and 'Stop! In the Name of Love'.

"We wrote for girls," Dozier explained. "A lot of the time I would have a conversation with girls and ask how they felt about this, that and the other. Or I'd be sitting in a restaurant in a booth, and I was a bit of an eavesdropper. There'd be people in the booth next to me—this happened a few times—and the girl would be crying and the guy would say: 'It's just over with. We just can't make it; I'm sorry'. And I'm just writing all this down …"

In general, sad music is thought to cause listeners to experience sadness, which is considered an unpleasant emotion.

However, scientific studies have shown that people may actually feel *positive* emotions when listening to sad music.

This was pretty much the message behind Elton John's 1983 hit, 'Sad Songs (Say So Much)'. Bernie Taupin's lyrics describe how it sometimes helps for someone who is feeling sad, or who has lost a partner, to listen to melancholic songs.

"I find sad songs comforting rather than depressing," says Australian/British singer-songwriter Natalie Imbruglia. "It makes you realize you're not alone in the world."

American country music singer-songwriter Reba McEntire agrees: "For me, sad songs often have a way of healing a situation. It gets the hurt out in the open into the light, out of the darkness."

US singer-songwriter Richard Marx—who wrote the classic rock ballads 'Endless Summer Nights', 'Right Here Waiting' and 'Now and Forever'—is also convinced that sad lyrics can have the greatest impact on listeners. "I don't find that there's much poetry in a successful relationship," he says. "The poetry comes from unrequited love and heartbreak … I just find that even as a listener I don't want to hear happy love songs, let alone write them."

American singer-songwriter Ingrid Michaelson (who co-wrote 'Winter Song' with Sara Bareilles) says she always looks for something sad even in a happy situation. She calls it "finding darkness in light".

British singer-songwriter Ellie Goulding takes a similar approach: "Even when I'm in quite a happy state of mind" she says, "I like writing really sad songs. I think a lot of people do."

However, the key to writing a successful sad love song is to be able to make the listener experience what you're feeling as the song progresses. But that doesn't simply mean describing your own emotions in your lyrics.

Instead of saying "I feel so sad …", you have to create those feelings in the listener. You can achieve this by telling a story that describes situations and circumstances and, in effect, explains the reasons for your sadness or regret.

Ideally, these reasons should be based on real-life experiences that everyone can relate to.

American singer-songwriter Pink—whose emotion-packed hits include 'So What', 'Blow Me (One Last Kiss), 'Who Knew' and 'Please Don't Leave Me'—believes that basing song ideas on what you've experienced in your own life tends to bring out the most authentic and relevant lyrics.

She suggests that new lyricists should think back to a particular situation that they have strong feelings about and use the memory of those feelings to inspire their lyrics.

"I would say to aspiring songwriters, as long as you're uncomfortable you're probably on to something," said Pink. "The more uncomfortable you are, and the more honest you're being, the better the outcome will probably be."

# # # #

#8
A TITLE NOBODY CAN REMEMBER

"The world is full of song titles"
—Bonnie McKee

MANY NEW writers don't realize how crucial a song title can be to the success of a song.

Their latest opus may contain their best-ever lyrics, but, if the title is weak and uninspiring, all those superb word choices they agonized over may never be heard by anyone apart from their friends and family.

In the same way that an eye-catching headline on a website or in a magazine can make you want to read the story, a distinctive, intriguing song title is often the best way to hook the interest of music publishers, A&R reps, record producers and radio programmers (and also record buyers if you're looking to sell your music direct to fans).

If someone else is writing the music and you're writing the lyrics, being able to come up with a memorable, attention-grabbing title could be your greatest contribution to the song.

According to some estimates, more than one million new songs are released every year. That's an awful lot of songs for you to compete with! But a captivating title can help you stand out from the pack.

Publishers and record labels' A&R departments receive hundreds of new demos every week and many music industry execs expect the majority of songs that come in from new writers to be unusable. Who can blame them if they have to forage through stacks of songs with uninspiring titles like 'I Love You' and 'I Miss You'?

You'll never get into the all-important 'must-listen-to' pile if your title is just like every other song in an A&R exec's morning mail.

It's also essential for your title to be easy to remember. It must be able to tell listeners what the song is about in just one word or in a single phrase that has no more than seven syllables. And to make the title unmistakable, it's important to avoid secondary phrases that might compete with it. This will make it easier for people to identify the title when they hear the song for the first time.

So what makes an outstanding title?

Experienced songwriters say short phrases or powerful single words—such as action words—tend to work best because they can convey a strong image (they also make effective Twitter hashtags and Google search words!).

Foo Fighters' Dave Grohl reckons writers should always treat their song titles like bumper stickers. His advice is: "Keep them simple, catchy and straight to the point".

Intriguing titles often come from putting words together that don't normally go together, such as 'Yellow Monday' or 'Frozen Sun'.

A significant new development for lyricists is the growing popularity of easy-to-remember, one-word titles—such as Adele's 'Hello', 'Happy' by Pharrell Williams and Ed Sheeran's 'Sing'.

A 2016 study by Priceonomics showed that, in recent years, there has been a steady upward trend in the number of one-word song titles in the *Billboard Hot 100*.

This could be a result of the growing importance of using catchy titles as hashtags to promote artists on Google, Twitter and other social media channels.

The Priceonomics study found that the probability of a one-word title is two and a half times greater today than in the 1960s (the average number of words per song title has also declined). In the 1960s, less than 10% of hit songs had a one-word title; today the figure is closer to 30%.

"There have always been songs with one-word titles, but in the first half of the 20th Century, they were uncommon," said Dan Kopf of Priceonomics. "If you peek at lists of popular songs from the 1920s and 1930s, you'll find that one-word song titles are exceedingly rare – hits like Jimmy Dorsey's 'Tangerine' and Billie Holiday's version of 'Summertime' are exceptions."

He added: "By the 1960s, one-word song titles were more popular, but still unusual, at less than one in ten hits. The growth was relatively gradual from the Sixties to the Nineties, and then accelerated at the turn of the new century."

Australian singer-songwriter Sia Furler is one of the finest contemporary exponents of the one-word title. She says she constantly uses her phone to keep a list of one-word titles that come to her.

This approach has resulted in a stream of highly distinctive songs such as 'Diamonds', 'Chandelier', 'Cannonball', 'Titanium', 'Reaper', 'Flashlight', 'Footprints', 'Opportunity', 'Alive', 'Unstoppable', 'Radioactive', 'Breathe', 'Invincible', and the incomparable Kylie Minogue hit, 'Sexercize'.

"I usually choose a word, one solid concept," explains Sia. "So say I'm looking around and I see a chandelier, I think 'oh, how can I use that?'. 'Chandelier' was a strong title because record labels want things that people can Google."

As Sia says, ideas for good titles can come from anything and everything around you. Inspiration may come from overhearing a conversation on a train or in a café … or an event that you witness … or while you're waiting at a traffic light. Similarly, a headline in a newspaper, on a website, or on a poster might spark an idea for a title.

So keep your eyes and ears open. Carry a notebook or use the voice memo option on your phone and always be prepared to grab a superb title idea when it floats past you.

# # # #

#9
NOT WRITING FROM THE TITLE

"I write from titles. I don't write the first line of a song. It's a mistake, because then you have to come up with the second one."
—Sting

ONE OF my most frequent disappointments as a music publisher is when I play a demo with a great title that has caught my attention, only to find that the writer has failed to deliver the storyline (and lyrical quality) suggested by the title.

There's no point in creating a distinctive, intriguing song title if you then fall short in writing the lyrics ...

As the late country legend Merle Haggard once remarked: "When your song is called 'XYZ' or whatever, every line has got to make sense against your title."

Publishers and A&R execs expect the title to encapsulate everything that a song is about. So your title has to be the emotional foundation of the rest of your lyrics—a stepping stone to your verses and the chorus.

That's why it is so important to write from the central idea contained in the title and build your complete lyrics around it.

According to 'MacArthur Park' songwriter Jimmy Webb, clarity is "the single greatest shortcoming" of new writers and their work.

"If a young songwriter doesn't really know what he wants to say, how the hell is he going to say it?" said Webb. "That's why I tell a lot of songwriters to start with titles."

As Jimmy Webb advises, taking your inspiration from the title can help you to focus and get you thinking in the right direction. And when you construct your song around an intriguing title, a lyric can sometimes almost write itself.

The legendary lyricist Sammy Cahn always believed that a good title can dictate the whole architecture of a song—with the words in the title helping to establish the cadence for the rest of the lyrics and consequently playing a part in determining the melodic structure. For example, the built-in rhythm and tempo of the syllables in the title can often be used as a motif to set up the hook in your chorus.

Experienced songwriters know that the title is the heart of a song. It's the foundation of the all-important hook in the chorus.

That's why many top writers don't even start working until they have a great title that moves them. They know that if they're not inspired by the title, then it's unlikely they'll be able to achieve an emotional connection with listeners in order to sell the song.

Once they have an exciting title, writing the rest of the song becomes a process.

As the Bee Gees' Robin Gibb once remarked: "We've written whole songs just from getting a title. 'You Win Again', 'Islands In The Stream', 'Woman In Love', 'Chain Reaction' and 'Too Much Heaven' all came that way."

Bernie Taupin—Elton John's longtime songwriting partner—almost always work off titles. "The majority of the songs I've written I've always thought of the title before I've written the song," he said. "I usually get the title on the top of a piece of paper, and I will start, basically, at the beginning, and work my way down. Sometimes I'll just write all the verses first and then come back and write the chorus. I never usually write the chorus first."

He added: "It's almost like I create a song like writing a story. The story comes alive."

Starting out by writing a mini-story based on your song's title is often an effective way to focus your creativity and make sure the title fulfils its potential.

Writing prose may seem like a non-musical way of crafting a hit lyric, but it could help you to really get inside your concept for the song and understand what it is you're trying to say (and, most importantly, what it is you want the listener to take away from the song).

Don't worry about laying your short story down in the form of lyric lines or rhymes. Just write it out as prose and construct your story.

The images and ideas inspired by the title can then be used to create interesting characters and situations.

And describing the physical experience of the characters' emotions—for example, by emphasizing senses such as sight, sound, smell, touch and taste—can often give you descriptive words, phrases or lines that you can later use to build the lyric itself.

####

#10

PUTTING YOUR TITLE IN THE WRONG PLACE

ANOTHER ASPECT of the craft of songwriting that many new writers overlook is knowing how to place the title line in the strongest possible position within their lyrics.

There's no point in creating a marvelous title if it flies past the listener's ears without them realizing it when they hear the song for the first time.

Putting the title in the most prominent position will make it much easier for people to recognize it and remember it. If the title is buried somewhere in the middle of the song it will have little impact and listeners may not be able to pick it out. So don't leave them guessing …

In today's highly competitive music market—where your song has to compete with so many others for airplay or prominence—the title is your strongest selling point and the best way to attract people's attention.

This applies whether you're pitching your song to a music publisher, a record label or a producer—or selling your music direct to fans.

Easy recognition of the title is an important commercial consideration. It means people who hear the song on the radio (or maybe during a scene from a TV drama series) will know what to look for if they want to stream it or download it, or if they want to buy it at a record store.

Trying humming your song without any lyrics and see how the melody leads you to a particular point where it feels natural to insert the title. This is most likely to be in the hardest-hitting part of the melody line ... the repeated hook motif in the chorus.

If your song has a Verse-Chorus structure, the most effective position is the first line or the last line (or both) of your chorus. This will allow the title to be repeated several times throughout the song like an easy-to-remember catchphrase.

With the Verse-Verse-Bridge-Verse format, the title should either be in the first line or the last line of the verse. One of the most famous examples of this is Paul McCartney's 'Yesterday'.

If you're using the more traditional verse-refrain structure (where the refrain is like a mini-chorus that is used to resolve and end a verse), the title should be placed in the two-line repeated statement at the end of a verse. An outstanding example of this is Paul Simon's 'Bridge Over Troubled Water'. The refrain at the end of each verse consists of the same line sung twice: "Like a bridge over troubled water I will lay me down".

Never put the title in the bridge or the pre-chorus section. The bridge usually only appears once in a song (typically somewhere in the middle).

The pre-chorus (also known as the 'lift') is normally only four bars long and its sole function is to propel the listener into the chorus. So your lyrics in the pre-chorus should light the fuse for the explosive title line when it appears in the chorus.

While it's generally accepted that the title has to be mentioned somewhere in a song, there are exceptions, of course. 'Unchained Melody' famously became one of the most recorded songs of all time despite not having the title anywhere in the lyrics.

At the other end of the scale, in Rihanna's 2012 hit single 'Diamonds'—written by Sia Furler and producers Benny Blanco and StarGate—the title is sung 35 times in three minutes and 45 seconds!

####

#11

NOT HIGHLIGHTING IMPORTANT PHRASES

NEW WRITERS often miss the opportunity to highlight the most important phrases or messages in their songs because they unwittingly put them in the wrong place in their lyrics.

They don't realize how vital it is to structure the lyrics in such a way that the phrases that matter most are emphasized by their location in the song.

In any lyric, there are always certain phrases or lines—usually in the verses—which contain essential information that will help listeners to see and understand what's happening in the song's story, and make them want to keep listening.

This means phrases that are core to the song's development (they aren't necessarily the most 'poetic' lines) need to be positioned where they are most likely to catch the listener's ear.

If this critical information isn't highlighted, the song's impact could be weakened when listeners (such as music publishers, A&R reps or producers) hear it for the first time.

There are several simple techniques which can be used to accentuate the most important strands of description or detail in your lyrics.

For example, if your verses have four lines, the most impactful place to put a pivotal phrase or a twist in your lyrics is on the fourth line of each verse. This also applies to a four-line bridge section.

As discussed later in this book, people have a subconscious desire for symmetry in all things—including the music they listen to.

As a result, a verse with an even number of lines is more satisfying to listeners' ears than a section with an unsymmetrical odd number of lines (such as three or five).

When listeners hear the fourth (or 'balancing') line in a four-line verse, it gives them a subliminal feeling of relief and reassurance and therefore attracts greater attention.

That's why the balancing line is the ideal location for the most important point you want to make in each verse.

A key phrase can be made even more impactful and memorable if it's placed in a balancing line that ends with an unexpected rhyme.

A highly effective way of achieving this is to rhyme words that don't have the same combination of letters but sound similar (for example, John Mayer rhymed 'knees' and 'breathe' in his 2006 song 'Dreaming With A Broken Heart'). This technique will make sure the important line really stands out and grabs the listener's attention.

Sound-alike words tend to engage people more than words with the same spelling because listeners derive a kind of delayed pleasure when they realize how the 'false rhyme' neatly matches up with the earlier line.

You can also accentuate an important phrase by making it part of a catchy internal rhyme that features two or more rhyming words within the same line (as in "The moon never beams without bringing me dreams" from Edgar Allan Poe's *Annabel Lee*).

Internal rhymes can be placed close together ("an ocean of emotion"), or further apart ("my tears of emotion could help fill an ocean") or even back-to-back ("a bottle of emotion lotion "). In a four-line verse, if you make lines 2 and 4 longer than lines 1 and 3, you'll have more scope for an attention-grabbing internal rhyme on the fourth (balancing) line.

Highlighting an important phrase by putting it in the right place in your lyrics could have other benefits too. Distinctive phrases from hit songs can often become items of intellectual property (IP) in their own right.

In 2015, for example, Taylor Swift moved to trademark some of the key phrases from her *1989* album to prevent them from appearing on unauthorized merchandise. They included lines like "this sick beat" (from 'Shake it Off'), as well as "nice to meet you, where you been?" and "party like it's 1989".

"If you have a three-word phrase, to be absolutely certain you get copyright protection if someone else uses just those three words, you want to go for a trademark," explained Alexander Ross, a partner at media, technology and IP law firm Wiggin. "Once you have a trademarked phrase you have the right to stop someone else using it on things like merchandising."

# # # #

#12
TRYING TO FORCE YOUR LYRICS

"Sometimes they come out easy, sometimes they don't come out at all... The ones that come out hard are usually the ones that aren't any good ..."
— Tom Waits

TRYING TOO HARD to make your lyrics happen rarely leads to great results.

Lyric lines that are labored often lack the emotion of something that comes to you naturally—like when you seem to just pluck a perfectly-formed idea out of the air (or, more accurately, out of your subconscious).

If nothing's happening during your writing session, leave it and go do something else. That's the advice offered by many experienced writers. They've found that switching to another activity often allows their mind to continue working on an unconscious level. Even taking just a short break can result in them hitting upon a great line that they couldn't find before.

"If you don't try and force it, a song will find the proper moment to come to life," insists Valerie Simpson who co-wrote classic songs such as 'Ain't No Mountain High Enough' and 'Solid (As a Rock)' with her husband Nickolas Ashford.

Irish singer-songwriter Hozier also believes in allowing a new idea to ripen in its own time. He says: "Sometimes you just kind of collect lyrical and musical ideas and don't actually complete the song until you feel like they work together and have a home."

Stephen Stills also advises against pushing things if you feel your efforts during a writing session are exhausted. "I sit down and start playing the guitar, if nothing comes I put it down," he says. "If something comes I pursue it until I get bored. I know better than to force it."

His former bandmate Neil Young takes a similar view. "If you don't have an idea and you don't hear anything going over and over in your head, don't sit down and try to write a song, go mow the lawn."

In other words, don't try to rush a new lyric. Be patient. Once you have a title or a concept, just let the words and phrases take shape in your subconscious, like a program running in the background on your computer.

Country singer-songwriter Mary Chapin Carpenter takes this approach a step further (literally). She clears her mind by going out on long walks in the fields near her home. "When I'm working on songs and I hit a block, I go what I call 'songwalking'," she told *Acoustic Guitar* magazine in 2016. "It's just another word for grabbing a dog or a cat and going out and riffing out loud what I've been working on as I walk. A lot of the time I find solutions on those walks, just singing over and over again until a solution comes to me."

When inspiration does come, don't stop the flow.

Don't let your inner critic begin to take over. Just take the lyrics that come instinctively and accept that they may change during the creative process.

And don't go chasing the 'perfect' rhyme or the correct phrasing—just get the first draft of the lyrics written.

If you spend too much time trying to perfect the wording of one line of the song, you could lose your connection with the spark that ignited the idea in the first place.

As The Bee Gees' Robin Gibb once remarked: "The worst thing is to try too hard. The minute you stop and give up for the day, the mind relaxes and suddenly something happens. I don't know why that is; it just feeds itself."

British pop and R&B songwriter Wayne Hector—best known for his work with Nicki Minaj and One Direction—believes it's just your mind telling you it needs a break. "A lot of people say 'carry on, write through it, break through that wall'. I don't believe in that at all," he told *The Independent*. "If your leg is in need of a rest, you stop running. Doing more on it will injure it further. For me it's the same thing with songwriting. Your brain tells you that you need a break and the first thing you do is stop and take time off. And when it's time, you'll start writing again."

The men and women in white coats agree. Scientists now believe a nap can boost creative thought. They've discovered that creative activity in the brain is highest during and immediately after sleep.

A study by researchers at the University of California in San Diego concluded that problems are more likely to be solved after a period of dreamy, rapid eye movement (REM) sleep. It appears that this kind of deep sleep allows the brain to form new nerve connections without the interference of other thought pathways that occur when we're awake or in non-dreamy sleep. In other words, dreams help to build remote links between information that our mind struggles with when we're awake.

This suggests that writers who start working earlier in the morning are more likely to come up with fresh ideas without having to force them. And if you're a night owl, you may be able to increase your creativity by taking a nap before you start a late-night writing session.

Anecdotal evidence indicates that there could be some truth in this. John Lennon once said that his song 'Norwegian Wood' came to him when he was trying to sleep. "I'd spent five hours that morning trying to write a song that was meaningful and good," Lennon recalled, "and I finally gave up and lay down. Then, 'Nowhere Man' came, words and music, the whole damn thing. You try to go to sleep, but the song won't let you. So you have to get up and make it into something…."

# # # #

#13

NOT TAKING STEPS TO AVOID WRITER'S BLOCK

"Before anything else, preparation is the key to success"
—Alexander Graham Bell

MOST SONGWRITERS have experienced the frustration of sitting down to write a new song, only to find that your ideas have dried up and nothing comes, or what you do manage to write just isn't good enough.

There can be many reasons for running into a mental roadblock from time to time. It happens to most writers. In 2015, a study of the causes of writer's block found that it is often triggered by writers' own high expectations and a fear of failure. Sometimes, it's just because your mind is on something else, or maybe you're worried about something.

Often, though, it's simply because you haven't prepared yourself properly for your writing session.

Experienced songwriters know that the creative process involves four key stages: (1) Preparation, (2) Incubation, (3) Inspiration, and (4) Realization.

Incubation is where an idea takes shape in your subconscious, like a program running in the background on your computer.

Inspiration is where an idea floats up from your subconscious and you seem to pluck it out of the air. And **Realization** is where the idea becomes a reality as you turn it into the first draft of a new lyric.

However, it is **Preparation** that is the foundation stone of the entire creative process. And being 'prepared' to write a lyric means much more than just keeping your laptop, digital recorder, smartphone and rhyming dictionary handy just in case.

In songwriting, 'creative preparation' is a state of mind. It means being observant and keeping your mind constantly open for new ideas through your experiences, thoughts, feelings and observations. It means keeping your writer's antenna switched on to the world around you at all times so you can cultivate a constant stream of concepts for lyrics.

An idea for a title or a lyric line can come from anything and everything around you. It could be a conversation you overhear on a train or in a café … or an event that you witness … or while you're waiting at a traffic light. Similarly, a headline in a newspaper, on a website, or on a poster might spark an idea for a song.

So always be prepared. Carry a notebook or use the voice-memo app on your smartphone to capture great ideas whenever you spot them.

As American singer-songwriter Nick Jonas told *Billboard* in 2016: "I'm inspired by everything I see. As I walk down the street there's always something that's going to catch my ear or my eye and inspire me in some different way. It's always about being open to receive whatever inspiration comes."

As you may have found already, one of the hardest things about writing lyrics is having to start with a blank page.

However, it is often easier to find inspiration if you have already laid the creative foundations by keeping a list of 'ready-made' ideas you can dip into. It could be a list of ideas for titles, or a collection of words and phrases (or even complete lines) that suddenly come to you based on your real-life experiences and observations.

When explaining her approach to songwriting, Sia Furler said: "Melody comes first and then I'll choose lyrical content from a list of concepts I have in my phone, and whenever I think of a new one I write it down. Then I'll just scroll through all of my notes and look for ideas …".

Taylor Swift revealed that the lyric for her 2014 chart hit 'Blank Space' was actually constructed from lines she'd been collecting for many years.

"Writing that song was a journey," she told music magazine *NME*. "I'll be going about my daily life and I'll come up with a line that I think is clever, like, `Darling, I'm a nightmare dressed like a daydream', and I'll jot it down in my notes. Then I pick them and put them where they fit [in the song] and construct the bridge out of more lines I've come up with in the last couple of years."

She added: "It was really more like a crossword puzzle. 'Blank Space' was like the culmination of all my best lines, one after the other."

Taylor Swift's 'crossword puzzle' approach is similar to Mark Twain's famous advice for trying to begin something new: "The secret of getting started," Twain wrote, "is breaking your complex overwhelming tasks into small manageable tasks, and then starting on the first one."

For a lyricist suffering from writer's block, this means taking the song you're struggling to write and splitting it into 'bite-size' chunks (for example, the title, the chorus, opening lines for verses, and the bridge).

First, identify the main point you want to make in each section of the song, then create a list of words or phrases that express what it is you want to say (ideally, they should be common, everyday words that you might use in a conversation with a friend).

A useful tip, which will be looked at in greater detail later in this book, is to keep your word ideas in separate columns—with narrative, descriptive words in your word list for the verses and more emotive words and phrases in your columns for the chorus and the bridge.

You may end up with dozens of words or phrases in each column. But, at this stage, don't think of them as lyrics; they're just markers or street signs that will give you directions when you start putting the song together.

Another way to try and overcome songwriter's block is to use the Jack Kerouac-style 'freewriting' technique to loosen your thoughts on a particular topic for a lyric.

Freewriting basically involves writing continuously for a set period of time (maybe five or ten minutes)—just pouring out all your thoughts and the images you see in your mind's eye without worrying about rhymes or making corrections or stopping to check your spelling and grammar. You just write whatever comes to mind, without any hesitation or self-censorship, until your allotted time is up.

Stephen Sondheim offers this advice: "The worst thing you can do is censor yourself as the pencil hits the paper. You must not edit until you get it all on paper. If you can put everything down, stream-of-consciousness, you'll do yourself a service."

The freewriting technique often produces material that is too raw and unusable, but it could still be worth reading your 'free words' out loud when you've finished. Your ear may pick up a rhythmic pattern or a neat idea that could work well in a lyric.

Many writers feel that, even if they end up with stuff they can't use, the whole freewriting exercise helps them generate enough creative momentum to liberate their minds and blast through any mental roadblocks.

In the 2015 study of writer's block mentioned earlier, researchers found that many professional writers managed to unblock their creativity through a combination of motivational techniques and daily routines. These included taking a daily 'walk and talk' break (using their phone's voice-memo app to record lyric ideas while they're out walking), or giving themselves a 'digital free' hour every day.

If you're one of those people who are addicted to social media, try switching it off for a while. You don't have to check Facebook, Twitter, Snapchat and all the other potential time wasters every five minutes. You won't miss anything. But your writing could gain a lot from the time you save!

In my experience, it's the writers who allow themselves to be distracted too easily who have the greatest difficulty when it comes to finishing songs that may bring them the success they long for.

Because they aren't focused, they can't sustain their interest ... the initial inspiration soon fades ... and their creative flow loses momentum.

Establishing a consistent writing habit—making it part of your daily routine—will boost your creativity and productivity, and lead to better lyrics. So it's important to challenge yourself to write something every day, even when you don't feel like it.

If you want to earn your living as a writer, it's important to remember that songwriting is a business—not a hobby. It's a job. The professional songwriters you will be competing with write every day, turning out at least 100 new songs a year.

So you need to do the same.

Identifying the most creative time of day for you is another way to avoid writer's block. Whether you're an early bird, an afternoon person, or a night owl, it's important to make your most fruitful hours your 'writing time', and get into the habit of sitting down and writing something at the same time every day (even if it's just for half an hour).

To maintain a daily writing schedule, it's important to find the ideal place where you can focus and be creative. If you write at home, it should be a clutter-free zone where you feel most comfortable—with no distractions. It needs to be a special place where you can close the door, turn off your phone, and give your mind the focused time it needs to get your creative juices flowing.

Once you identify the best 'prime time' for you and start writing, you'll find you're a lot more productive. And you'll be amazed how the quality and volume of your lyrics will improve as a result.

# # # #

#14

TRYING TO SAY TOO MUCH

"My theory of writing is to write a song that has a complete idea and tells a story in the time allotted for a record"
—Smokey Robinson

WRITERS WHO are just starting out often feel they have to cram as much as possible into a song in order to impress music publishers, A&R reps or record producers.

But if you really want your lyrics to pack a punch, you should concentrate on just one strong message or emotion …and build your song around it.

After coming up with a first verse and chorus, you may feel compelled to move on to a different topic in the second verse, and maybe another new theme in the bridge. But, far from impressing people, presenting multiple ideas in this way can have the opposite effect.

Many aspiring writers understand that a good lyric needs to create images in the listener's mind, but they often go overboard with their descriptive language. Be creative, but be concise in your phrasing.

Your lyrics should make one major point, from one point of view, with a mixture of skillful (but succinct) emotional descriptions and clear everyday language.

Even if you want to express a range of emotions, make sure there's a single unifying theme that brings it all together—such as a specific situation that the narrator or the characters in the song find themselves in—so that all of your words can work towards one main idea.

If you try to explore too many ideas or themes, there's a danger that you'll send out mixed messages to the listener. The last thing you want is to confuse people so much that they end up losing interest in the song.

To prevent your lyrics from going off in too many directions, you need to be clear about the whole point of the song before you start writing.

You should be able to describe what the song is about in one short phrase (in the movie world, it's known as the 'high-concept').

Most established songwriters believe simplicity is an important common denominator in all successful songs. The unwritten rule is:

—Don't say more than you need to, and say what you need to say as concisely and clearly as possible.

—Don't write too many verses when, with some self-discipline, your story could be condensed and told in two or three high-impact verses.

Country singer-songwriter Lucinda Williams says she learned her sense of concision from her father, the American contemporary poet Miller Williams. "Dad stressed the importance of the economics of writing," she told *Rolling Stone* magazine. "He'd say 'clean it up, edit, edit, revise'!"

Removing any unnecessary words will make the lyric more focused and easier for listeners to understand.

And it may resonate more powerfully with them as a result.

# # # #

#15
PLAYING IT TOO SAFE

"A lot of people from my generation of music are so focused on playing things correctly or to perfection that they're stuck in that safe place."
—Dave Grohl

NEW WRITERS often tend to play it safe and don't attempt to stimulate a response within listeners by slipping in occasional left-field rhymes and lyric lines that can take people completely by surprise—for example, by bravely adding a couple of intriguing phrases that make listeners stop and think, or ask questions.

Just one thought-provoking line can often hook people in and keep their attention throughout the song. If you can make an impression on listeners in this way, your song is more likely to stick around in their memory.

One song that achieved this kind of impact was Jimmy Webb's enigmatic 1967 song 'MacArthur Park' which famously included the line *"someone left the cake out in the rain"* as a metaphor for lost love. In a 1982 interview, Webb told *Rolling Stone* magazine: "People appear to have developed an incredible fascination with that one image of the cake out in the rain."

Another lyric line that has had a similar effect is Paul Simon's reference to baseball legend Joe DiMaggio in his 1968 song 'Mrs. Robinson'. In the middle of a description of the life of a middle-aged woman, the lyric suddenly asks (seemingly out of context): *"Where have you gone Joe DiMaggio?"*. There has been much discussion about the meaning of this line ever since.

Perhaps the greatest 'what does it mean?' song is 'Ode to Billie Joe', written by Bobbie Gentry in 1967. The meaning of the Grammy-winning song still mystifies listeners today. There are even countless blogs devoted to theories about the song's haunting and mysterious lyrics.

'Ode to Billie Joe' contains two lines that have always captivated listeners: *"Billie Joe McAllister jumped off the Tallahatchie Bridge"* and the revelation that Billie Joe and a girl were seen *"throwin' somethin' off the Tallahatchie Bridge"*. What Billie Joe and his girlfriend threw off the bridge and why Billie Joe killed himself are not explained in the four-minute song.

'Ode to Billie Joe' is like a gothic novel written in only 350 words. Its first-person narrative tells the story of two Mississippi teenage lovers who share a dark secret that eventually leads to the boy's suicide. The cryptic lyrics are made even more powerful by including the dialogue of the female narrator's family at dinnertime on the day that Billie Joe jumped off the bridge. Throughout the song, the suicide and other tragedies are contrasted against the banality of everyday routine and polite conversation.

In a 1967 interview about the song, Bobbie Gentry said: "Everybody...has a different guess about what was thrown off the bridge—flowers, a ring, even a baby. Anyone who hears the song can think anything they want ... but the real 'message' of the song, if there must be a message, revolves around the nonchalant way the family talks about the suicide."

She added: "They sit there eating their peas and apple pie and talking, without even realizing that Billie Joe's girlfriend is sitting at the table, a member of their family."

You can also surprise an audience by mixing everyday words with a few abstract lyric lines full of symbolism designed to stimulate the listener's imagination.

But it's important to take care not to go over the top and make the lyrics too 'arty' or avant-garde ... otherwise you could end up alienating listeners if the lyrics become too inaccessible.

As a music publisher, I remember going to see a new, young rock band who sounded great and had an exciting stage presence. I asked them to send me some of their songs.

One of the tracks they provided contained highly cerebral lyrics about anti-gravity and the use of magnetic levitation to move vehicles around. The song was never going to be a hit, of course, but the lyrics certainly made me stop and think ... and I've never forgotten it!

Most lyrics touch listeners by conveying creative descriptions of tangible objects or emotive situations.

However, abstract writing can also make a strong emotional connection by requiring the listener to think deeply in order to conjure up a thought or a mental image.

Without doubt, the finest exponent of this conceptual approach was David Bowie.

Bowie often came up with intriguing lyric lines by employing the 'cut-up' writing technique used by postmodernist author William S. Burroughs in his controversial *Nova Trilogy*—a series of experimental novels written in the early 1960s.

'Cut-up' is a literary technique designed to add an element of chance to the creative process.

It was developed by applying the montage method used in art to the creation of words on a page. It involves taking finished lines of text (such as phrases from a newspaper or a magazine), then using a pair of scissors to cut the selections into pieces.

The resulting fragments are then rearranged at random to create a brand new text.

The cut-up concept can be traced back to the 1920s when the Dadaist art movement in Europe laid the groundwork for abstract writing and sound poetry. The technique was developed further in the early 1950s by painter, writer and sound poet Brion Gysin—and then popularized in the early 1960s by Burroughs.

This technique also influenced Kurt Cobain's cryptic lyrics. In fact, the Nirvana frontman even had a chance to meet and collaborate with Burroughs.

Cobain once remarked that he didn't like to make his songs too obvious so that they wouldn't become stale.

"My lyrics are total cut-up," he said. "I take lines from different poems that I've written. I build on a theme if I can, but sometimes I can't even come up with an idea of what the song is about."

Thom Yorke is also said to have applied a similar method when writing the lyrics for Radiohead's 2000 album *Kid A*. He reportedly wrote single lines, put them into a hat, and drew them out at random while the band rehearsed the songs.

In a 2008 interview, David Bowie explained: "I use the [cut-up] technique for igniting anything that may be in my imagination and I can often come up with very interesting attitudes to look into."

He said: "You write down a paragraph or two describing several different subjects, creating a kind of 'story ingredients' list, I suppose, and then cut the sentences into four or five-word sections; mix 'em up and reconnect them."

He added: "You can get some pretty interesting idea combinations like this.

"You can use them as is or, if you have a craven need to not lose control, bounce off these ideas and write whole new sections."

After David Bowie released his album *The Next Day* in 2013, a journalist asked him to explain his thinking behind the new songs, each of which featured unusual, cryptic lyrics and surreal imagery.

Bowie responded by sending the journalist a list of 42 words which supposedly provided the framework for the critically-acclaimed album.

Those 42 words were:

Effigies ... Indulgences ... Anarchist ... Violence ... Chthonicum ... Intimidation ... Vampyric ... Pantheon ... Succubus ... Hostage ... Transference ... Identity ... Mauer ... Interface ... Flitting ... Isolation ... Revenge ... Osmosis ... Crusade ... Tyrant ... Domination ... Indifference ... Miasma ... Pressgang ... Displaced ... Flight ... Resettlement ... Funereal ... Glide ... Trace ... Balkan ... Burial ... Reverse ... Manipulate ... Origin ... Text ... Traitor ... Urban ... Comeuppance .... Tragic ... Nerve ... and Mystification.

Quite a surprising lyrical framework for an album that ended up including song titles such as: 'The Stars (Are Out Tonight)', 'Love Is Lost', 'Where Are We Now?', 'Valentine's Day' and 'The Next Day'!

# # # #

#16

WEAK CHARACTERIZATION

"When I'm writing a song, I try to be the character."
—Stephen Sondheim

MANY NEW lyricists tend to start writing as soon as an idea comes to them and they finish the song without realizing that they haven't fully developed the central character.

Listeners are left with only a blurred image of the song's protagonist—whether this is the narrator/singer of the song or the character (or characters) that the narrator is singing about.

While it's important to get your ideas down as quickly as possible so you don't forget them, rushing to complete a lyric can often result in weak characterization.

If people can't get a clear picture of the character in their mind when they listen to the song, it'll be much harder for them to relate to the character and the story.

Your song will be much stronger—and have a far greater impact on listeners—if you can deliver a distinctive, believable character that people can easily visualize and identify with. This will also help listeners to react emotionally to the situation the character is in.

You can't just leave it to the music to provide the characterization. Experienced songwriters know that the melody and chord progressions can set the scene by supplying the mood, feel and emotional foundation of the song. But, just like a dramatist writing a three-minute play, it's the words that people hear that will ultimately help them to understand the character through what he or she says, sees, does or thinks.

So whatever emotions you're looking for listeners to experience, the music can provide the emotional canvas, but you still have to paint your word pictures on that canvas in order to bring your character and story to life.

As mentioned earlier, it's very tempting when that initial burst of inspiration hits you to get right into the song. By all means, quickly write down all the words and phrases and lines that float up from your subconscious so you don't lose them. But it's a good idea to then sit back and think more deeply about the character (or characters) in your story. Get to know and understand him or her or them, so you can fine-tune and strengthen your word choices.

This will help to make your lyrics richer and more deeply layered in order to enhance listeners' perception of the character and the story.

There are two different approaches to characterization: the direct approach (where you tell the audience what you want them to know about the character), or indirect characterization (where your lyrics show the audience different aspects of the character to give them an understanding of his or her personality and emotional state … and how these factors relate to the song's story).

There are five basic methods of characterization: physical description, action, inner thoughts, reactions, and what the character says.

You must first understand all of these character traits yourself before you can effectively convey them to the listener.

That's why it's worth taking a little time to firm up the character (or characters) that the song is about before you really get into the song. Who are they? What's happening to them? What emotions do you want to evoke in listeners when they hear the story?

If the character is imaginary, bring him or her to life by making a list of words that describe the character. For example, make a note of the character's gender, age, clothing, body type, hair color, hair style, physical traits (tall, slim, short, overweight), personality traits (introvert, extrovert, logical), lifestyle traits (urban, rural, blue-collar, white collar), idiosyncrasies, flaws ... even how the character moves.

The more specific and detailed you are in your description of the character, the more real the character will become.

You may not end up using any of this stuff in your lyrics, but such details will help you to build a multi-dimensional image of the character in your own mind. This should help you to paint richer word pictures which, in turn, will make it easier for listeners to 'see' the character when they hear the song.

If the character is the narrator of the song, how does he or she talk? What is the character's motivation or state of mind? In order to match the character's mood and personality, should your lyrics be conversational (including slang)? Or snappy? Full of attitude? Ironic? Humorous? Melancholy? Anxious? Angry?

Feel what your character is feeling. Visualize yourself in the scene and see the situation through the character's eyes. This will help you to understand what he or she is going through. By writing 'in character' in this way, you'll be able to create a more emotional song because you've gone much deeper into the story and into the mindset of the character.

Award-winning American songwriter Diane Warren always likes to put herself in the shoes of the character she's writing about. "I see pictures in my mind and become the character in the song as I'm writing," she says. "It's kind of method songwriting, where you're the actor in the song … I can't say that I actually live what I write, but I know what people think and feel so I write those feelings the best that I can."

Becoming your character—in effect, pretending to be someone else—can put your head in a completely new place which may often inspire phrases and ideas you hadn't thought about when you got the initial idea. Sia Furler even describes her songwriting approach as "play-acting" (hence the title of her 2016 album *This Is Acting*).

"Lyrically, if I only stick to my own personal experience, I'm limited," says American singer-songwriter Richard Marx. "So sometimes I put myself in a scenario that's happened to someone close to me. I've even made a first-person story out of a scenario I've read in a book or seen in a film."

The US electropop singer-songwriter Halsey says she gets her characterization ideas by basing her songs on real people. "There is nothing more interesting than the people around you—the people in your life that have affected you."

# # # #

#17

NOT MAKING SENSE OF YOUR SENSES

"Although you're writing about an experience which only you have had, you're trying to welcome other people into it. One of the ways of doing this is through the senses, through the sounds and the smells."
—Ronald Frame

MANY NEW writers don't pay enough attention to developing sensory writing skills that can enrich their word pictures and help them bring their lyrics to life.

They often don't fully appreciate how sensory language can inspire vivid descriptions that will help them express a human experience or create realistic, emotive images in the listener's mind.

As mentioned earlier in this book, nothing establishes a stronger connection with listeners than powerful imagery that engages the five physical senses: seeing, hearing, touching, tasting and smelling.

You can also help listeners feel what you're feeling by describing internal sensations (such as butterflies in your stomach, an ache of disappointment in your chest, or the dryness in your throat because you're nervous).

Similarly, conveying a feeling of body motion (swaying on the deck of a boat in rough seas, or hurtling towards the ground on a rollercoaster) can also help listeners to share the experience.

Each of these senses can impact on an audience's perception of a song and add greater depth to the lyrics.

That's why sensory writing is far more powerful than simply stating facts. When done well, it can help to make sensations seem 'real' in the listener's imagination.

The more sense-related words and phrases you use to describe a situation or the central character's feelings, the more you'll put the listener right in the middle of your song. Then they can be part of the experience too. And descriptions that draw on multiple senses in the same lyric line can be very powerful.

The English Romantic poet John Keats (1795-1821) is regarded as the standard bearer of sensory writing.

As one of the original Romantics in the early 19th Century, Keats developed a unique style that was more heavily loaded with sensual imagery and emotion than any poet who had come before him. His poem 'The Eve of St. Agnes' is considered to be one of the finest early examples of sensory writing.

Benjamin Haydon, the 19th Century English painter and a great friend of the poet, wrote that Keats was moved to an unusual degree by sensory identification with things around him.

"Nothing seemed to escape him," Haydon wrote. "The song of a bird and the undertone of response from covert or hedge, the rustle of some animal ... The humming of a bee, the sight of a flower, the glitter of the sun, all seemed to make his nature tremble."

Keats's writing contains many sensory devices that all work together to create rhythm and music in his poems. Although lyrics aren't the same as poetry, of course, all of Keats's sensory techniques can be exploited to great effect by songwriters. And creating rich, sensory lyrics that are original and meaningful could help to define you as a writer.

So how can you incorporate the five senses into your lyrics?

SIGHT

Sight is the sense most frequently used by songwriters to develop their song's story, scene by scene.

You can create an enhanced visual description of something by using metaphors or similes to compare how an object looks in relation to something else. These are important tools for bringing lyrics to life and making it easier for listeners to picture the scene in their own way, based on their own past experiences.

Another method of adding visual details is to give a description of a specific hue or shade (not just the basic color). For example, a sunny blue sky could become "a warm expanse of pale azure". Objects can also be described by alluding to shapes or patterns.

Describing the brightness or darkness of a setting can also help to match the mood of the melody and chord progression. The Eagles' 1976 song 'Hotel California' is a great example of this. It contains visual lines such as: "On a dark desert highway…" and "Up ahead in the distance I saw a shimmering light…".

In 2008, Don Felder—The Eagles' guitarist and co-writer of 'Hotel California'—described how the lyrics came to be written. "Don Henley and Glenn Frey wrote most of the words," he explained. "If you drive into L.A. at night... you can just see this glow on the horizon of lights, and images start running through your head of Hollywood and all the dreams that you have, and so it was kind of about that …".

SOUND

You can also bring your lyrical setting to life by describing the sounds that you (or the character in the song) can hear all around. Maybe a church bell ringing in the distance, a child crying, the slap of water on a boat hull, or the wind rustling the leaves.

Put yourself in the character's shoes and 'hear' what he or she might be hearing (for example, "her fragile sobbing tore my heart apart"). Make a list of specific verbs (also called 'action verbs' or 'vivid verbs') that can add extra vitality to your description of the sound.

TOUCH

Describing what something feels like can add an extra dimension to your lyrics—and you have five million sensory nerve receptors (and over twenty different types of pain nerve endings) to choose from!

A listener's tactile sense will be able to relate to any description of touch that involves hands, lips, face, neck, hair, tongue, fingertips or feet.

It could be the feeling of a jilted lover's eyes stinging from salty tears, or a warm breeze kissing someone's cheek as they drive with the top down. In The Eagles' 'Hotel California', Don Henley sings about feeling the "cool wind" in his hair while he's driving.

Imagine all the textures or surfaces that you (or the character) might come into contact with as the song unfolds. You can describe the roughness, smoothness, coarseness or fineness of these textures. You may also be able to trigger an immediate response from listeners by using similes, metaphors and analogies to compare a touch sensation to something that is already familiar to them.

In other words, use vivid descriptive words to convey how the touch sensation feels in order to bring listeners into the song so they can experience it for themselves.

TASTE

Most people have a strong sense of taste. Whether it's something bitter, sweet, salty or sour, it is one of those experiences that tends to etch itself deep into someone's memory.

That's why bringing a familiar taste into a lyric line can be a great way to engage listeners.

It could be the tingling sensation of an ice-cold cola on a hot summer's day … the sweet taste of a fresh, juicy orange … or a mouthful of freshly baked bread that reminds you of home and your mother's cooking. Everyone can relate to taste images such as these.

And if your imagination can stretch to taste descriptions beyond food and drink—such as the bitter taste of salt in the air on the beach—then you could really surprise listeners with your lyrics.

SMELL

The sense of smell is perhaps more closely linked with memory than any of the other senses. As perfumers know only too well, a fragrance can be highly evocative.

That's why it's a great way to stimulate a specific emotion within listeners by tapping into their memories.

Describing a familiar smell—such as smoke from a homely log fire, or the aroma of freshly brewed coffee—can create a picture in the listener's mind of a particular moment in his or her life.

Certain smells can also instantly remind people of a person from their past—such as the perfume or cologne worn by an old girlfriend or boyfriend.

If your sensory description of a particular smell can make a connection between your lyrics and the listener's own experiences, then you've got them hooked.

American singer-songwriter John Grant's 2013 song, 'Pale Green Ghosts', was inspired by the scent of the Russian olive trees that he used to drive past late at night on the I-25 highway in Colorado.

The olive trees' fragrant, luminescent leaves are the 'pale green ghosts' of the title. The song includes the line: "Pale green ghosts must take great care, release themselves into the air".

You can also use a sense of smell to suggest a mood or a setting.

For example, the line "warm smell of calitas rising up through the air" in 'Hotel California' is said to be a reference to the Mexican slang term for the buds of the cannabis plant—so this line is effectively providing a glimpse of the marijuana-influenced, 'hippie' lifestyle of 1970s California.

After you've incorporated the five senses into your writing, go back through your lyrics and highlight each instance of sensory detail. Perhaps use a different colored marker for each sense. This will allow you to see at a glance if your use of sensory sketches is balanced throughout the song.

When listeners hear the sense-bound language in your lyrics, it may encourage them to start filling in the details from their own imagination … drawing them deeper into the heart of your song.

# # # #

#18

TELLING NOT SHOWING

"All you can write is what you see"
—Woody Guthrie

ONE OF the most frequent mistakes in lyric writing is trying to evoke a strong emotional response in listeners simply by stating what you're feeling or thinking (for example, "I'm getting mad" or "I'm feeling down").

This is actually one of the *least* effective ways to make a lasting connection with the people who hear your song.

In the verse lyrics especially, you need to show listeners what the song is about by painting vivid word pictures that describe the physical experience of the emotions you want to convey.

In other words, invite the audience into the world of your song by allowing them to "watch" the story unfold like a movie. Hal David always believed that a song should be "like a little film told in three or four minutes".

By describing each scene as if you're looking through the lens of a video camera, you'll be able to help people 'see' and experience what the performer of your song is feeling.

Legendary singer-songwriter Joni Mitchell has always taken a highly visual approach to her lyrics. "My style of songwriting is influenced by cinema," she once explained. "It's very visual. I'm a frustrated filmmaker. You're scoring the actress, but the actress is singing the lines and trying to get them as conversational as film."

She added: "A fan once said to me, 'Girl, you make me see pictures in my head!' and I took that as a great compliment—that's exactly my intention."

Irish singer-songwriter Chris de Burgh takes a similar approach with his lyrics. "I tend to view my songs in a very filmic way," he said. "They're like movies for the ears."

He added: "I allow my mind to run riot with the images—and the great part about all this is trying to get that sense of imagery over to the listener."

As explained in the previous chapter, one of the best ways to show listeners what's happening—and help them experience your story for themselves—is to include sensory details based on the five physical senses: seeing, hearing, touching, tasting and smelling.

A description comprised of sensory detail can penetrate layers of the listener's consciousness and deepen the emotional power of a song.

Another effective 'show' technique is the use of action words—usually vivid verbs—that express a specific emotion by describing what the character is doing when he or she feels that emotion.

You don't need to tell listeners how the character is feeling because they can 'see' it for themselves from your choice of verbs.

For example, in a line such as "She slowly wiped a tear from her cheek and smeared it across her face", the words "wiped" and "smeared" are the vivid verbs.

A line such as "I yelled back at the angry sky" shows the listener what your state of mind is in the song.

Similarly, you can use a description of a character's body language to show what's going on inside his or her head.

This device enables the character's inner feelings, thoughts and intentions to be expressed by describing physical behaviors, such as facial expressions, body posture, gestures and eye movement.

While listeners can't see 'sadness', for example, they can see the body language and actions that show that a person is sad. For instance: "Silently, she caressed the pale band on her finger/where her wedding ring once used to be …".

You can also help listeners to enter your song by including descriptions of familiar, tangible objects in your lyrics—such as an empty chair, a wine glass, a framed photograph, and other concrete nouns which refer to physical entities that can be observed by at least one of the senses. These images are more likely to engage listeners than a dull statement of fact.

Tom Odell's beautiful song 'Constellations'—from his 2016 album *Wrong Crowd*—opens with Tom talking to a girl in a busy bar and his lyrics vividly describe the scene.

"In order to write that," Tom Odell told Dale Kawashima of *SongwriterUniverse* magazine, "I had to imagine every detail in that bar—the picture on the wall, the girl's voice, the jacket on the back of the chair, the gentle hum of the bar, the chair that squeaks, the look on her face. I almost have to live it in my head in order to write the song. But obviously you can't get all of that detail in the song. You can only pick a few of those details to sing."

Other 'show' devices that can create visual representations of ideas include:

—**Personification** (relating actions of inanimate objects to human emotions—for example, "The stars leaned down and kissed her lips").

—**Similes** (describing someone or something by making a direct comparison with something else, usually with the help of the words 'like' or 'as').

—**Metaphors** (describing one thing in terms of another, or, as Aristotle defined it, giving something a name that belongs to something else).

In David Guetta's dance classic 'Titanium' (co-written with Sia Furler, Giorgio Tuinfort and Nick Van De Wall), the singer metaphorically compares herself to one of the strongest metals on the planet. The metaphor shows that no matter what anyone throws at her, or how much they try to break her, they won't succeed.

Personification can also be used to give your lyrics a deeper meaning. People naturally look at the world from a human perspective, so it's easier for an audience to relate to something that is human or possesses human traits.

Using personification to give human characteristics to non-human things can add extra vividness to your lyrics, and give listeners a better understanding of what you're feeling or seeing in your head.

Owl City's 2008 song 'Fireflies' (written by Adam Young) contains the wonderful line: "I get a thousand hugs from ten thousand lightning bugs, as they try to teach me how to dance". Young described the personification in the lyric as "a little song about bugs and not being able to fall asleep at night."

As mentioned previously, the use of similes also helps to create vivid, attention-grabbing word pictures that make it easier for listeners to understand the meaning of a lyric line as it flashes past in the song. For example, Taylor Swift's 2011 song 'All Too Well' (co-written with Liz Rose) includes the clever simile: "You call me up again just to break me like a promise".

And Katy Perry's self-empowerment anthem, 'Firework' (co-written in 2010 with Mikkel S. Eriksen, Tor Erik Hermansen, Sandy Wilhelm and Ester Dean) contains no less than eight powerful similes—including the lines "Do you ever feel like a plastic bag?" and "Just own the night like the fourth of July", as well as the title line: "Baby, you're a firework ... Come on, show 'em what you're worth".

The inspirational simile in the title line insists that everyone is like a firework because they're special and capable of astounding the world.

# # # #

#19
UNCONVINCING CHOICE OF VERBS

"If you are using an adverb, you have got the verb wrong"
—Kingsley Amis

MANY BEGINNING songwriters make the mistake of peppering their lyrics with adjectives and adverbs and fail to pay enough attention to their choice of verbs.

They don't realize that how they use verbs in a lyric can often make the difference between a great song and an average song.

Experienced songwriters know that strong, descriptive verbs create much better imagery for listeners and therefore have a greater emotional impact. That's why many writers believe well-chosen verbs are the most important element of any lyric.

As the Pulitzer Prize-winning American journalist and author J. Anthony Lukas once observed: "If the noun is good and the verb is strong, you almost never need an adjective."

Putting a greater emphasis on verb-based writing is particularly important because verbs largely control the power, clarity and personality of each line. For example, impactful, monosyllable verbs like 'sting', 'cry', 'creep', 'yell' or 'snap' can help to drive the rhythm and pace of a lyric.

This is very important if you're pitching your songs to music publishers and A&R reps. They're busy people and ear-catching verbs can keep a lyric interesting and may help to hold their attention for longer.

Almost every Bob Dylan lyric, for example, is comprised of active verbs that are rich and vivid. He doesn't waste an opportunity to use every verb as a way to convey action, drama, conflict and motion in his songs.

A simple but effective way to improve your writing is to avoid overused verbs such as 'put' 'get' and 'went', and also replace 'to be' verbs (which are weak) with strong verbs. For example, instead of "I got there by morning", you could say "I raced through the night".

Using too many stative verbs (such as 'am', 'feel', 'want', 'like', 'sit' and 'stand') can also weaken a song and make the lyrics sound dull. This is because they usually express a state of being and are static or unchanging. Replacing them with dynamic verbs which describe a specific action can result in lines that are more powerful and therefore more likely to engage listeners and stimulate their senses.

That's why choosing the most precise verb possible to describe an action is essential to effective lyric writing.

Remember, every single word counts when you're writing lyrics. You only have a limited amount of space in which to work (typically 15-20 lines). So you have to convey your message in as few words as possible.

You can often deliver a more descriptive line with fewer words by using a vivid action verb (such as "he raced" instead of "he ran quickly").

Dynamic verbs express a wide range of actions that may be physical ('jump', 'run', 'hit', 'break'), mental ('ponder', 'question'), or perceptual ('see'). They help to paint compelling mental images that can draw listeners into your lyrics. They bring nouns to life and are more powerful and precise when you need to create an engaging, descriptive line that shows how a particular action is completed.

Instead of settling for the first verb that comes into your head, though, use a thesaurus to find the strongest, dynamic verb which will precisely describe the action or emotion that you want to convey.

Then take a pair of scissors to many of the adjectives and adverbs that you thought you needed to tell your story!

And, whenever possible, try to use the active voice ("I drove the car") instead of the passive voice ("The car was driven by me").

In other words, always put the action in the verb.

Using a strong, active verb at the heart of a lyric line will make the line more concise, less awkward in construction, and much easier for the listener's ears to grasp.

# # # #

#20
WHERE'S THE DETAIL?

"Describing all the little details of a situation can make a song a lot more interesting. It can give it heart and soul and make people feel something"
— Bonnie McKee

NEW SONGWRITERS often get so carried away by the exhilaration of hitting on a new idea that they rush headlong into finishing the lyrics.

In their own minds, they can see the song's story unfolding and they can feel how the character in the song feels. But they often don't stop and ask if they're presenting enough detail to help the listener see those pictures and feel those emotions too.

While taking care not to fill your lyrics with over-flowery language—or make the song too long—it's essential to supply enough concrete detail to show exactly what is happening on the 'screen' in your mind.

This will help the audience to visualize it more clearly for themselves.

And using familiar, everyday words in descriptive phrases, similes and metaphors can make your lyrics much easier for listeners to follow in real time.

A few extra details can often make the difference between a generic lyric that only puts a blurred, monochrome image in the listener's mind, or a lyric that generates a dynamic mental picture in full-color, high-definition 3D!

The inclusion of lines filled with vivid pictures will help to make your lyrics more distinctive and memorable whatever genre you're writing in.

This is especially true in your verse lyrics.

As you will read later in this book, the song's story is most often told in the verses. Each verse should move the storyline forward like a new chapter in a book, pulling listeners into the song by introducing fresh information and images that will spark their imagination and captivate them.

That's why the lyrics in your verses should be mostly descriptive (giving details about people, places and events) so that listeners can 'see' and understand what's happening as the story grows.

"I feel that writing songs is kind of like describing a dream," the American singer-songwriter Bonnie McKee once remarked. "You go into great detail about how did it feel? What did it look like? What were you wearing? Where were you? What did you hear? What did you smell?"

One way to make sure you have a clear idea of the messages that you want to convey in your lyrics is to follow the advice of British poet and novelist Rudyard Kipling (1865-1936). His secret to good writing is set out in his famous 1902 poem, *The Elephant's Child*.

Kipling's much-loved poem opens with the words:

"I keep six honest serving-men
They taught me all I knew
Their names are What and Why and When
And How and Where and Who."

Asking yourself these six questions about your song's central character, storyline and overall message will put you in a better position to provide the more detailed descriptions that may be needed in your lyrics.

For example:

—**What** is the main message that you want to convey in the song?

—**How** do you want listeners to feel when they hear the song?

—**Who** is the song about?

—**When** does the song take place?

—**Where** does the song take place?

—**Who**'s talking?

—**Who** is he or she talking to?

—**What** is the central character doing?

—**How** is the character feeling? What is their mindset?

—**Why** is the character doing or feeling what he or she is doing or feeling?

—**What** happened to trigger the events or attitudes in the song?

—**What** can the character see, hear, touch, taste and smell?

—**What** is the central character wearing?

—**Who** else is in the song?

—**What** are other characters doing, wearing, saying, etc.?

The more What? Why? When? How? Where? and Who? questions you ask yourself, the clearer the images will be in your own mind. It will help you to see the big picture of your song.

You'll be able to hear the voices of the song's characters more clearly, and feel the emotional substance of what they're saying more intensely.

You may not use all of this information in your lyrics, but clarifying your thoughts in this way will enable you to be much more creative with the descriptive details that you need to convey to the listener.

Top songwriter/producer Nile Rodgers believes that trying to find the DNA of each song in this way is essential if it's going to work.

"The meaning of each song has to be clear to me," he told PRS For Music's *M Magazine*. "If I can't explain it, then how can [listeners] understand it?".

But don't be tempted to simply include a list of facts in your lyrics.

As explained in Chapter #18, don't just tell listeners stuff. You have to *show* all of these details in the form of mental 'pictures' so you can engage the listener (whether the listener is a publisher, an A&R exec or a record-buyer) … and then hold their attention through to the end of the song.

# # # #

#21
NOT KEEPING YOUR IMAGERY SIMPLE

"The creative process is imagination, memories, nightmares and dismantling certain aspects of this world and putting them back together in the dark. Songs aren't necessarily verbatim chronicles or necessarily journal entries, they're like smoke"
—Tom Waits

SOME NEW writers often make the mistake of using over-elaborate imagery, or deliberately opaque abstract phrases, in an effort to show how clever and creative they can be. Unfortunately, what they sometimes end up with is a collection of clumsy lines that simply sound pretentious and self-indulgent.

Far from being impressed, music publishers and A&R reps are more likely to view superfluous flowery language and exaggerated descriptive phrases as a sign of inexperience.

Dictionaries typically define 'description' as "a means of transmitting a mental image or an impression". As mentioned in the previous chapter, it's important to include enough descriptive detail in your lyrics to be able to paint a picture in the listener's imagination so you can stimulate their senses, reach them on an emotional level, and make them feel what you're feeling (or what the singer is feeling).

But new writers often tend to overcook their figurative language and make descriptions too wordy or rambling.

They don't realize that the way in which detail is conveyed can play a big part in the success or failure of a song. It's one of the most challenging aspects of the craft of successful lyric writing.

Remember, you only have three minutes or so in which to get some concrete images and vivid colors onto your lyrical canvas to captivate listeners.

This often means having to manipulate descriptive devices such as metaphor, simile and personification within the constraints of a clearly defined song structure and rhythm. And, as if that isn't hard enough, you also ideally need to get to the all-important hook lyric in the chorus within 45-60 seconds from the start of the song!

That's why many top writers' lyrical language tends to be much simpler, more concise and more down to earth—with short lyrical images and carefully-chosen descriptive phrases that are easily understood and can therefore connect with the listener's ears immediately.

Experienced lyricists know that going overboard with descriptive language can sometimes detract from the most important emotions in a song. By using common, everyday words in an imaginative way, it's possible to craft realistic images and impressions that connect with listeners and lets them participate in the song.

Keeping your imagery simple in this way can also make a song easier to remember when people hear it for the first time.

Award-winning country singer-songwriter Brad Paisley believes songwriters should always think of the images their words will create in listeners' minds when they're writing lyrics.

"My idea of music is always about the pictures it paints for you," he says. "I don't like songs that don't give me images in my mind."

# # # #

#22

SAYING THE SAME OLD THING IN THE SAME OLD WAY

"Say something in a way that hasn't been heard before. That's what makes a great lyric."
—Brett James

COMING UP with new ways to describe feelings in order to create an emotional response within listeners is one of the biggest challenges for lyricists.

Unfortunately, some writers take the easy way out and end up recycling the same themes and emotional cues again and again—telling each story from the same perspective every time, instead of trying to find a fresh and unique way to express what they want to say.

Filling lyrics with words, phrases and descriptions that you've used before could be seen by publishers and A&R execs as a sign of lazy writing or, even worse, limited talent.

If they like a demo you sent them and ask to hear more of your work, they're likely to spot any recurring imagery, metaphors and similes in the additional songs you submit.

Respected English singer-songwriter Richard Thompson gives this advice to new writers: "Copy everyone except yourself ... It's important to keep searching, and not go for the obvious idea."

Even when you have a strong, attention-grabbing title, if you use it as the foundation of a storyline that's been told a thousand times before ("my lover left me" or "my life's a mess"), the song may still end up being rejected.

Publishers and A&R reps listen to a huge number of songs every week and I know from my own experience as a publisher that it can often be a fruitless search for originality.

If music industry pros know where your lyric is going from the moment it starts, they're likely to hit the 'stop' button right away.

That's why it's so important to try and surprise listeners by freshening things up and writing from an unexpected perspective—perhaps turning a song on its head and telling a familiar story but from a totally different angle or point of view.

For example, the Norwegian singer-songwriter Aurora wrote about a murder from the *victim*'s perspective in her chilling 2015 song 'Murder Song (5, 4, 3, 2, 1)'. The lyrics include the line: "He holds the gun against my head. I close my eyes, then bang! I'm dead."

In his critically acclaimed song 'Stan', Eminem wrote about fan adoration from the perspective of an obsessive fan. The song tells the poignant tale of a young guy (Stan) who claims to be Eminem's biggest fan.

Stan writes a series of letters to the singer, becoming more and more obsessed and angry with his idol when he doesn't receive a reply. Finally, Stan is so incensed that he creates a voice recording of himself driving his car off a bridge into a lake, with his pregnant girlfriend in the trunk. The first three verses are delivered by Eminem as Stan while the fourth verse is Eminem as himself attempting to reason with the troubled young man.

Written in 2000, 'Stan' is now recognized as one of the greatest hip hop songs of all time.

If you usually write in the first person (I, me, mine), your lyrical idea may be even stronger, fresher and more distinctive if you put your actor's hat on and tell the story through someone else's eyes.

For example, instead of saying "Do you still love me, baby?" the story could be told from the point of view of that person's best friend.

A notable example of this was The Beatles' 'She Loves You' which was the first song that John Lennon and Paul McCartney wrote from a third-person perspective. It proved to be a turning point in their songwriting partnership.

"I suppose the most interesting thing about ['She Loves You'] was that it was a message song," Paul McCartney told author Barry Miles in the book, *Many Years From Now*.

"It was someone bringing a message," McCartney explained. "It wasn't us any more, it was moving off the 'I love you, girl' or 'Love me do'. It was a third person, which was a shift away. 'I saw *her*, and *she* said to me, to tell *you*, that *she* loves you' … So there's a little distance we managed to put in it which was quite interesting."

According to lyricist Dean Pitchford, the lyrical concept behind Melissa Manchester's 1982 hit 'You Should Hear How She Talks About You' (co-written with Tom Snow) was borrowed from 'She Loves You'.

"It was the idea of somebody reporting to somebody else on hearing this girl's in love with you, or this boy's in love with you," Pitchford explained.

Re-working your lyric in the second person (you, your, yours) may also help you to come up with some imaginative lines because it means you're addressing the audience (or a specific person) directly.

For example, in Taylor Swift's 2010 song 'Dear John' she uses the lyric as an 'open letter' to an ex-boyfriend. It includes the clever line: "Long were the nights when my days once revolved around you".

Other inventive second-person songs include Joni Mitchell's 'Big Yellow Taxi' ("You don't know what you've got till it's gone") and Bob Marley's 'Redemption Song' (which includes the line: "Emancipate yourselves from mental slavery").

As well as taking time to consider the most impactful form of narrative for your latest song, you could also avoid saying the same old things in the same old way by broadening your range of vocabulary.

A 2015 study by MusixMatch.com found that the average vocabulary of most songwriters is around 2600 words.

To determine which top writers use the widest range of language, MusixMatch analyzed the lyrics of the 100 densest songs (by total number of words) written by best-selling writers across 25 genres.

The study found that Eminem has the biggest vocabulary in music (8,818 different words used across 100 tracks), beating Jay Z (6,899 words) and Bob Dylan (4,883 words).

How does your vocabulary compare with these writers?

# # # #

#23
TOO MANY CLICHÉS

*"Most lyricists rely too much on the standard clichés.
Good writers turn the clichés around"*
— Aimee Mann

WHEN MUSIC publishers, A&R executives and producers listen to a demo of a new song, one of the most common reasons why they end up hitting the 'stop' button is because they find the song's lyrics are too full of clichés.

The English novelist George Orwell once described clichés as "dying metaphors" which, he said, tend to be used because they save writers the trouble of inventing new phrases for themselves.

Some lyricists are often tempted to fall back on the same old metaphors, similes or other figures of speech when they find themselves struggling to come up with something truly original—especially when faced with the challenge of having to say so much in only a few bars of music.

Resorting to clichés can be an easy way to reduce your word count because these timeworn phrases are so familiar to listeners that you don't have to explain what they mean. But using too many tired clichés can make your song sound corny and trite, even when you're trying to be genuine and honest.

It's important to remember that by the time music industry pros get to hear your demo they've probably already listened to thousands of songs during their careers. So they literally have heard it all before.

They've had to endure all the old worn-out lines ("can't live without you", "standing the test of time", "don't rock the boat") as well as overly familiar descriptions, tired phrases, threadbare metaphors, and predictable rhymes (such as "kiss you...miss you").

Many of these phrases were originally created by great lyricists, of course, but they've been reused and misused so many times over the years that they've now become boring clichés that lack depth and have lost their evocative power. In effect, they've reverted to being just like an ordinary word.

If someone is going to sign your song, or cut it with their artist, they want to hear lyrics that are fresh and inventive … with some original rhymes or a new twist on an old theme.

Don't forget, when you're trying to attract the attention of producers and A&R reps, you're going to be competing with songs by the world's most successful writers.

That means your song has to be more unique and compelling than theirs.

So avoid clichés … unless you can find a way of twisting them into new shapes that nobody has heard before.

One of the finest examples of turning a cliché on its head is Diane Warren's song 'Un-Break My Heart' which was a huge hit for Toni Braxton in 1996.

The phrase 'break my heart' must have been used thousands of times since the dawn of 'popular' music in the mid-19th Century. But Diane Warren used it to create something brand new that really made the song stand out.

"The phrase 'un-break my heart' just popped into my head," she explained, "and I thought, 'I don't think I've heard that before, that's kind of interesting'."

American singer, songwriter and producer Ryan Tedder—responsible for global hits such as 'Halo' by Beyoncé, 'Burn' by Ellie Goulding and Adele's 'Rumour Has It'—says even when he already has a concept, a verse and a melody, he's still constantly seeking the killer phrase and trying to avoid clichés whenever possible.

"I always try to find the clever way to say something," Tedder told *The Guardian* newspaper. "Let's say the concept of a new song is that I'm madly in love with you and I'm free-falling from a 60ft building, and then at the end I say: 'And I don't want a parachute' ... You need that turn of phrase."

The best way to avoid using clichés is to provide as much concrete detail as you can in as few words as possible. A few extra details—coupled with some vivid verbs—can often make the difference between a bland, generic lyric and one that creates a dynamic mental picture that helps the audience feel the emotions you're trying to stimulate in them.

The takeaway from this is: if there's a line or a phrase that you want to use and you've already heard it in other songs, push yourself hard to find a new way of saying it.

If you can come up with something out of the ordinary, it's likely to have a far greater impact ... and create a much stronger image in the listener's head.

And never be afraid to turn to a dictionary or a thesaurus for help and inspiration.

# # # #

#24

NOT TAPPING LISTENERS ON THE SHOULDER

"My first line is always something I know to be completely true, such as an image or an emotion ... It's supposed to let the listener in on something."
—Tom T. Hall

ALTHOUGH A song's title is its strongest selling point and the best way to attract people's attention, many inexperienced writers don't realize that the lyrical content of their song's *opening line* can play an equally important role in stimulating the listener's interest and creating a lasting impact.

It's like tapping a stranger on the shoulder and saying: "Hey, listen to this ...".

While the title should tell people what your song is all about in just one word or a single phrase, the lyrics in the opening line of the first verse should be just as memorable and interesting. A strong opening line can pull people into a song and keep them listening.

As Jimmy Webb explained in his fascinating book, *Tunesmith - Inside the Art of Songwriting*: "The first line must pique the listener's curiosity ... It is the songwriter's counterpart to the first few lines of a three-act play in miniature."

If you're aiming to write a song with commercial potential, it's important to understand how little time you have to grab the listener's attention at the beginning of the song.

Recent scientific studies—designed to unlock the secrets of what makes music memorable—have highlighted the importance of getting your first line right, and making it instantly recognizable.

One experiment by the UK's Museum of Science and Industry (Mosi) found that songwriters may have less than five seconds to hook an audience.

The study revealed that The Spice Girls' 1996 hit, 'Wannabe', has the catchiest and most memorable first line in chart history ("Yo, I'll tell you what I want what I really really want ..."). Music fans participating in the online experiment were able to recognize the song in just 2.3 seconds, compared with an average of five seconds for other songs.

The same time frame applies when you're pitching a song to busy publishers, A&R executives or producers. When they play your demo and hear your opening line for the first time, they're already deciding whether or not to hit the 'stop' button.

So you only have a few seconds in which to convince them to keep listening.

Ideally, the first line should set the scene and paint a vivid picture that will really draw the listener in. It should stimulate his or her imagination, and pave the way for the story that follows. A good example of this is The Bravery's 2007 song 'Believe' which opens with the evocative first line: "The faces all around me don't smile, they just crack …".

How many classic songs have stuck in your mind over the years because you remember the first line of the lyrics as well as the title line?

It could be a catchy opening line like "Well, she was just seventeen – you know what I mean" (from 'I Saw Her Standing There' by The Beatles) … or an intriguing metaphor or personification like Paul Simon's "Hello, Darkness, my old friend" (from Simon and Garfunkel's 'The Sound of Silence') … sensory imagery such as "On a dark desert highway, cool wind in my hair" (from The Eagles' 'Hotel California') … an emotionally-charged line like "I could stay awake just to hear you breathing" (from Diane Warren's 'I Don't Want to Miss a Thing') … or an imaginary telephone call like Adele's "Hello, it's me. I was wondering if after all these years you'd like to meet …".

A play on similar word sounds can also be effective, such as Little Richard's classic "A-wop-bom-a-loo-mop-a-lomp-bam-boom" from 'Tutti Frutti' (described by *Rolling Stone* magazine as "the most inspired rock lyric ever recorded").

Engaging first lines such as these instantly draw listeners into a song and hook their interest.

Listen again to a few songs by your favorite writers and make a note of the opening line in each case. Analyze the structure of the line and the writer's choice of words. See how it works like a mini hook and sets the stage for the rest of the song. Then apply what you learn to the first line of your own lyrics.

# # # #

#25

FAILING TO SUPPORT THE SONG FORM

NEW WRITERS often don't realize that the different sections in the popular verse-chorus format (verse, pre-chorus, chorus and bridge) have very different responsibilities.

As a result, these writers fail to support the song's overall shape and form by not carefully crafting their lyrics to reflect the important variance between each section.

If you listen closely to the lyrics of today's most successful songs, you'll find that the verses mostly use descriptive words (telling a story, describing people and situations, or showing the singer's state of mind).

Meanwhile, the chorus lyrics mainly deliver an emotional outpouring (of joy, despair, pain, anger or frustration) in response to the verses.

Look on the verse-chorus song structure as a roadmap, with the verse as a scenic highway that offers lots of interesting sights along the way ... the pre-chorus—located between the end of a verse and the start of the chorus—is like an interchange or a ramp that takes you off the highway and closer to your destination ... and the chorus is your exciting journey's end.

The pre-chorus (also known as a 'lift') is typically only four bars long and is designed to add a burst of extra energy at the end of the verse. Its function is to suddenly propel the listener into the chorus.

Pre-chorus lyrics should therefore combine verse-like descriptions with something more emotive to prepare listeners for the soaring emotional release in the chorus.

Meanwhile, the lyrics in the bridge—which usually comes in after the second chorus—should provide new material to contrast with your messages in the verses and the chorus (almost like saying "but on the other hand ..." when you're in the middle of a conversation with a friend).

Your main focus in the verse, therefore, should be to use descriptive words in a linear and conversational way to set the scene and then move the song's storyline forward towards the main message in your hook.

Balance your lyrics by saving strong emotions for the chorus.

As you drive toward the chorus, you can introduce fresh information and images in each verse to attract and hold the listener's interest.

First verses usually provide the broad strokes necessary to set the stage for the rest of the song, while the subsequent verses can be more specific.

The chorus, meanwhile, is the section where the whole point of your song should become clear and memorable.

You should be able to use simpler and more emotional words in the chorus because the verse has already built a firm foundation and filled in all the details—allowing the chorus to focus on hammering home the title and the all-important hook line.

####

#26

A LYRICAL HOOK THAT DOESN'T STICK

"If you listen to the songs I write, they are the most ADHD songs ever. They have five hooks in one and it all happens in three minutes."
—Will.i.am

THE HOOK is meant to be a simple line that is so catchy musically and lyrically that it immediately grabs the listener's attention and gets inside his or her head.

But writers who are just starting out often create hook lyrics that are too long and too complicated for listeners to remember easily.

You can't just produce a few words for the title line in your chorus and call it 'the hook'. If the melody and lyrics don't stick in the listener's mind, it's not a hook. And many music publishers and A&R reps may reject a song if the hook doesn't have 'stickability'.

So what makes one set of words catchy, pleasing and easy to remember, while another string of words may sound awkward, contrived or dull?

It's hard to define what makes a lyrical hook 'catchy' and 'sticky', but it generally comes down to the sequence of sounds produced by the words you choose and the way the syllables rub together in conjunction with the melody. In other words, it's all about crafting a short phrase that brings connected syllables and melodic sounds together to create a line that is instantly memorable.

Skillful use of alliteration (the repetition of a particular sound in the stressed syllables at the beginning of adjacent words) can make a hook lyric catchier and easier to remember—especially if you're looking to create a sing-along or anthemic hook.

For example, Taylor Swift's song about lost friendship, 'Bad Blood', is a simple but effective example of alliteration in a hook. The title line says: "Baby, now we've got bad blood ...". Repetition of the 'b' sound in 'baby', 'bad' and 'blood' adds to the memorability of the hook.

Listen closely to the hooks from some of today's biggest hits and you'll hear how simple and short they are. More than half of all hit songs have a hook phrase less than three words and four beats long.

You'll also hear how successful writers make their hook lyrics even more memorable by repeating them many times throughout the song. The more they repeat the hook, the more it sticks.

When you're writing a lyrical hook, remember that simplicity goes hand in hand with repetition. The song's title is the only information you need to include in the hook. The song's story should be told in the verses.

It is also important to build instant familiarity into the words used in a lyrical hook. That's why many title line hooks are derived from sayings, phrases and casual words that we hear every day. Something so familiar is reassuring to the listener and, subconsciously, makes the song easier to follow—increasing its 'stickability'.

And keep in mind that the last line of your chorus is the most powerful position in the whole song. It's the last thing the listener hears before your lyric returns to telling more of the story in the next verse.

For this reason, the final line of the chorus is the perfect place to put a lyrical hook that is more likely to stick in the listener's mind …

# # # #

#27
NOT USING THE BRIDGE TO ADVANCE YOUR STORY

NEW WRITERS often don't make full use of the bridge (or 'middle eight') in their songs because they don't understand the true purpose of this section.

They make the mistake of treating it as a throwaway segment that is simply there to give listeners a brief release from the verses and the chorus (or to make the song longer!).

The bridge is usually positioned immediately after the second chorus, and the bridge lyric typically sits on an eight bar melody and chord progression that is not heard anywhere else in the song.

Inexperienced writers often use this break simply to re-state what has already been said elsewhere in the song (albeit in a different way with a few word changes).

To gain the most from the bridge section, though, it should be treated like a mini-song within the main song.

The bridge lyric has a number of very important tasks—all of which have to be achieved within a musical time-span that is roughly the same length as the chorus … about 30 seconds!

The main purpose of the bridge is to add extra impact—and sustain the listener's interest—by building on the lyrical drama created in the verse and chorus.

It should therefore add crucial new information to the storyline—perhaps delivering an unexpected twist or a new revelation to contrast with what has already been said.

It can also be used to set things up lyrically for the big climax at the end of the song.

In other words, the bridge should advance the storyline and intensify the emotion—perhaps surprising listeners by changing the lyrical cadence and even the rhyme pattern ... or by taking the lyrics in a completely different direction.

It's also important to note that a well-written bridge lyric should be both descriptive and emotional. It should contain a succinct combination of the observational style of the verses and the emotional energy of the chorus.

But don't make the mistake of treating the bridge like another chorus. Don't use it just to hammer home the title line. To avoid confusing listeners, the bridge should never include the song's title ... always keep the title in the hook in the chorus for maximum impact.

# # # #

#28

TOO LITTLE REPETITION
(OR TOO MUCH)

ONE OF the most significant features of today's hit songs is the heavy use of repetition.

Certain lyrical phrases are deliberately repeated throughout the song to make it sound instantly 'familiar' and therefore much easier for listeners to remember.

Studies have found that people often feel more comfortable listening to a song they already know, or when they hear a new song that sounds kind of familiar.

This element of familiarity is especially important when relying on radio airplay and streaming services to help 'break' a new single.

Record labels and publishers know that most songs require multiple radio plays over several weeks in order to climb the charts—so repetition of key melodic phrases and lyrics (especially the title line in the chorus) is a powerful way to firmly plant the song in listeners' heads.

Repeating rhythmic patterns of syllables in a lyric can also play a big part in making songs singable and easy to remember.

A repeating syllabic motif is the equivalent of a melodic hook. But new writers often struggle when it comes to finding the right balance between repeating lyrical phrases often enough to help make the song memorable ... and using too much repetition which can make the song sound trivial and boring.

Too little repetition and you can't hold listeners' attention ... too much repetition and you turn people off ... and no repetition at all can make your lyrics sound far too dense and complicated to be remembered easily.

That's why your songs need to have a good balance of surprise and predictability (through repeating patterns) ... without overdoing one or the other.

To figure out how successful writers manage to achieve this fine balance, take time to analyze some of today's biggest hit songs. Pick out the words and phrases that you hear repeated again and again in the same lyric. You're likely to find that, these days, many songs frequently feature about 10 repeats of the title line throughout the song.

Make a note of how and where the repeated phrases are used in each song—and apply a similar template to your own lyrics.

You'll probably find much more repetition of rhythmic lyrical phrases in choruses than in verses. That's because the verse's job is to convey detail and paint word pictures for listeners, so it doesn't need to be particularly memorable—just compellingly visual. A good chorus, though, is built on repetition ...

# # # #

#29

INCONSISTENT VIEWPOINT

"Between each album I try to gain a new insight that I didn't have before and perhaps write a song about something that I've written about before, but from a fresh viewpoint."
—Don Henley

SOME DEVELOPING songwriters run the risk of baffling listeners by not being consistent in their use of pronouns, such as 'I', 'me', 'we', 'us', 'he', 'she', 'them', 'they' and 'you'.

Without realizing it, they jump from one to another during the song and consequently don't maintain the same point of view throughout their lyrics.

Switching pronouns in mid-song can make your lyrics unclear and may cause you to lose focus. And if the viewpoint of your song keeps changing, there's a danger that listeners will end up getting confused about what's happening—and may simply switch off.

Ultimately, it is you, the writer, who controls what the listener feels, sees and hears through the perspective you choose.

So when you start working on a new lyric, it's important to decide upfront which viewpoint the singer is meant to take when performing the song.

Will the singer be singing about himself or herself … or singing about someone else … or singing to someone else?

As mentioned previously in this book, it is essential to clarify your thinking by asking yourself questions such as: "Who's talking?" and "Who is she or he talking to—and why?"

It's also important to consider which point of view will help you to present your lyrics in the most compelling way.

For example, you may decide to turn the song on its head and tell your story from a totally different angle than the norm.

In most cases, though, the point of view tends to be determined by whichever character has the most at stake in the song.

The viewpoint you select will then dictate which personal pronouns, subject pronouns and object pronouns should be used throughout the song.

A first-person lyric ('I', 'we', 'me', 'us') is told from the perspective of the singer who is talking directly about himself or herself.

The lyrics portray exactly what the singer sees, feels or experiences. It allows the listener to hear only the point of view (opinions, thoughts and feelings) of the singer and nobody else.

A second-person lyric involves the singer referring to the song's main character using second-person pronouns, such as 'you', 'your', 'yours' and 'yourself'.

Traditionally, the second-person form is used less often than the first-person and third-person. However, one of the best contemporary examples of a second-person lyric is Adele's 'Someone Like You' (co-written in 2010 with Dan Wilson). It includes the line: "I heard that you're settled down/That you found a girl and you're married now ...".

Writing a lyric from a third-person perspective ('he', 'she', 'it', 'they', 'them') is the most objective narrative form because it involves the singer telling someone else's story from the outside looking in.

This approach provides a lyricist with the greatest flexibility because you're not directly involved in the action. You're not conveying your own feelings or experiences. You're writing purely as an observer and story-teller ... and the performer of the song is a narrator.

The most common mistake is when a writer takes a third-person perspective in the first verse (singing about someone else, but not directly to them) and then in the second verse shifts either to a first-person narrative ('I', 'we', 'me', 'us'), or to a second-person viewpoint (singing directly to a specific person).

If you take a third-person perspective in the first verse ('He did this' or 'She did that'), then all subsequent verses (and the chorus!) should also have a third-person viewpoint.

These days, many songs tend to be in the first-person, with the singer talking to someone else in a conversational style. A song becomes much more personal and intimate when 'you' and 'I' are used.

Whichever viewpoint you choose, however, it's essential to keep your pronouns consistent. Make sure each character in the song is represented by the same pronoun each time, both in the verses and the chorus. Listeners may get confused if, in the middle of the song, someone who was previously addressed as 'she' suddenly becomes 'you', or if 'he' becomes 'me'.

One occasional exception, though, is in the bridge. Some experienced writers deliberately change the viewpoint in the bridge as a means of adding something fresh to the song. But be careful not to cause any confusion if you do shift the lyrical perspective in this way.

Remember, simplicity and clarity are essential. So it's usually best to stick to a single viewpoint throughout the song, and always make it clear who is doing the talking or thinking.

# # # #

#30

LOSING YOUR BALANCE

"The chief forms of beauty are order and symmetry ..."
—Aristotle

SCIENTISTS SAY practically all laws of nature are based on symmetries, and symmetry is deeply ingrained in humans' inherent perception of everything—from physical objects ... to the shape of people's faces ... to the music we listen to.

Whether we realize it or not, a set of lyrics with a well-balanced shape and form can help to meet this subconscious desire for symmetry. Even line lengths and syllable counts help to create a sense of predictability that is reassuring and a source of comfort for the listener.

While some writers construct songs based on short lines of lyrics, others have longer lines with more phrases and syllables. There is no fixed rule. However, the English poet James Fenton—a former Professor of Poetry at Oxford University—reckons a line is "at its most relaxed and manageable" at around 10 syllables. Composers say it is usually much easier to write a good melody for a lyric that has shorter lines.

Whether you go short or long, what you should never do is make the mistake of using a different line length or syllable count in the corresponding line in each verse or chorus! It's the same as ensuring that all your verses have exactly the same number of bars and your pre-chorus and chorus melodies are the same length every time the listener hears them.

Any imbalance in lyric lines can affect the sense of symmetry that is very important to listeners' ears (whether the listener is a music publisher, an A&R rep, or an ordinary record buyer). If your song lacks this essential symmetry, it may subconsciously influence an audience's opinion of the song.

The symmetry and predictability of a well-balanced shape will make it easier for listeners to follow your song when they hear it for the first time.

It will also allow you to establish a solid base on which you can then create a few lyrical surprises without taking listeners too far out of their 'comfort zone'.

For example, you could build the dramatic tension towards the end of the song by putting an extra phrase in the last line of the last verse as it catapults into the chorus repeats.

When you analyze the structure of your favorite writers' songs, you'll find they usually have the same number of syllables between corresponding lines.

In other words, if the first line of their first verse has eight syllables, then the first line of their second verse will also have eight syllables.

Similarly, if their verse or chorus consists of four lines, then every verse or chorus will have the same number of lines, and each line will have the same number of syllables.

This may be because an even number of phrases and syllables in each section tends to create a feeling of stability in the listener, whereas an odd number could make the lyric sound awkward and may create a distracting imbalance for people who hear the song.

Award-winning Swedish songwriter, producer and hit machine Max Martin is known for putting a firm emphasis on the way an identical number of syllables can underpin a melody.

One of Max Martin's songwriting partners, Bonnie McKee, has described his approach to syllables as "very mathematical".

"A line has to have a certain number of syllables," she said, "and the next line has to be its mirror image … If you add one syllable, or take it away, it's a completely different melody to Max. I can write something I think is so clever, but if it doesn't hit the ear right then Max doesn't like it."

# # # #

#31

TOO MANY WORDS

TRYING TO squeeze too many words into a lyric is one of the most common mistakes made by inexperienced songwriters—especially writers who aren't singers themselves. They don't realize the importance of leaving pauses between the words so that the poor singer can grab a breath!

If your lyric lines are too crowded, singers will be so busy trying to fit all the words in that they won't have space to emphasize the key words—and won't be able to interpret the song in their own distinctive way.

Putting too many words into a song will also make it harder for listeners to take in the lyrics and understand what the song is about. It's like someone talking so fast that you can't grasp what they're saying. People have to be able to make out every word you've worked so hard to craft—otherwise, what's the point?

Being able to say a lot in as few words as possible is part of the craft of successful lyric writing. The great lyricist Hal David was a master at conveying what he wanted to say in the most concise way possible, despite the complexity of some of Burt Bacharach's melodies.

As Paul Simon told *American Songwriter* magazine: "When you're reading poetry, you read it at a much slower pace. So the lines can be much denser and have words which are not usually in a speaking vocabulary and which carry multiple meanings. But in a song, it's clocking along, and if you missed it, it's gone. And if you miss enough of it, well, the song is gone …".

You may be able to reduce your descriptive word count by experimenting with creative devices such as metaphor, simile and personification. These 'poetic' tools don't have to involve long, abstract ideas. By using everyday words and phrases, you can keep them simple and conversational yet still expressive enough to make listeners feel the emotion or see the picture that you want to convey.

Sia Furler and David Guetta's "I am titanium" and Katy Perry's "You're a firework" are good examples of simple yet effective metaphors.

Even if you're not a great vocalist, try singing your lyrics yourself at the intended tempo for the song. Or read the lyrics out loud rhythmically, keeping time as if you were singing them. If you can't fit all the words in comfortably—while emphasizing the key words—it's likely that an experienced singer won't be able to do it either.

In other words, if your lyrics are a maze of words, it will be hard for any performance of them to be amazing—especially on your all-important demo of the song.

If you find your lyric lines have ended up too word-heavy, it's time to do some ruthless editing ...

# # # #

#32

NOT ENOUGH CONTRAST BETWEEN VERSE AND CHORUS

WHEN WRITING in today's most common song structure—verse-chorus-bridge—new writers often come up with a distinctive song title and an intriguing theme, but then go and weaken the overall structure of their lyrics by not including enough contrast and tension to make each section of the song sound different from the other segments.

As a result, the verses, chorus and bridge can end up sounding too much alike.

There's no variation between them and no built-in tension and release.

It's similar to driving a shiny new car on a long, straight road with no trees or scenery and no bumps in the road. The car may look great but the journey itself can soon become boring for the passengers.

Similarly, a song that remains on the same level throughout its journey can leave listeners feeling unsatisfied—especially if there are no lyrical signposts along the way to spark the listener's interest and point them towards their ultimate destination … the chorus.

And if listeners can't tell where the verse ends and the chorus begins, the journey may seem endless.

As stated earlier in this book, it's important to remember that the different sections of a song serve different purposes.

It is these differences that can hold listeners' attention and help them distinguish between the verse, chorus and bridge. The changes also enable you to surprise listeners and stimulate their interest at crucial points in the song.

So how should verse, chorus and bridge lyrics differ from each other in order to add contrast and variation?

Chapter #25 explained how you should make sure you alternate between descriptive and narrative phrases in the verses and more emotive lyrics in the chorus and bridge.

Shifting between these two different types of lyrics can create an extra level of contrast which will strengthen the musical differences that already exist in the melody and the chord progression.

Since each verse usually features the same melody, it's the responsibility of the verse lyrics to advance the story and build the tension.

The verses have to give the song substance by setting the context, telling an interesting story, introducing fresh detail, and describing people, places and events with imagery that will captivate the listener.

In sharp contrast, the chorus should set itself apart from the verses by delivering the song's main message in the form of a passionate emotional outburst that releases all of the tension built up in the verses. This surge of emotion is meant to drive home the whole point of your song—for example, by frequently repeating the title line like a catchphrase.

You can also help to emphasize the chorus by making the rhyming pattern of the chorus lyrics—and even the cadence of the syllables—substantially different from those in the verse. The verse may be filled with meaningful words (with more notes per beat), but the chorus lyrics should be lighter and less crowded.

To achieve the greatest contrast and impact, therefore, the chorus needs a simpler and tighter meter, fewer syllables, and longer notes to help its more emotional lyrics register with listeners.

All of this means the information conveyed in the chorus can be much more general and philosophical, making it easier for people to remember the words.

Meanwhile, the bridge section is where you can give your song an extra lift and take it to another level to finish the story. The most emotional lyrics tend to come in the bridge where the story is being resolved, or where you're adding an extra twist in the tale to heighten the emotion.

The rising and falling emotional layers built into the structure of your lyrics should help to pull listeners into your song and keep them interested during the song's journey.

Once you've achieved this, your shiny new car will be racing up and down hills on an exciting, undulating road … surrounded by a picturesque landscape full of vivid imagery … with plenty of sharp twists and turns along the way to keep the passengers interested (and eager to make the same journey again!).

# # # #

#33
NOT ENOUGH METRIC VARIATION

ASPIRING WRITERS who come up with a great idea for a song sometimes fail to build on the song's potential (often without realizing it) because they end up making all their lyric lines the same length.

And they unwittingly put the same number of syllables—and a similar pattern of stressed and unstressed syllables—on every line.

Just like someone reciting the exquisite words of William Shakespeare in a dreary monotone, a lack of metric variation in the structure of your lyrics can make a potentially good song sound boring and monotonous … and may result in listeners losing interest.

As mentioned earlier in this book, an impression of symmetry is necessary to give a song a cohesive feel and to create a sense of predictability that is reassuring for the listener.

However, there is also a danger in being *too* predictable.

If the lines in your verses, bridge and chorus are all shaped the same—with an identical lyrical rhythm—it can be hard to create a sense of progress as the song moves forward.

And this apparent lack of direction in the song is unlikely to impress music publishers, A&R execs and record producers.

So what is 'metric variation' and why is it so important?

To understand the value of metric variation, it's important to first appreciate that all song lyrics have a rhythmical structure of their own (even without the music). This is because lyric lines are constructed from the basic building blocks of all language: *syllables*.

In English, most one-syllable words are stressed, and all words with two or more syllables have a primary syllable that is stressed, followed (or preceded) by syllables that are not stressed. This is what creates the sonic shape of a word.

The meter of a song (spelled 'metre' outside North America) is the number of syllables in each line of a song and the way in which those different syllables are arranged into a pattern of stressed and unstressed sounds (beats and offbeats).

Some books about the theory of lyric writing devote page after page to technical descriptions of meter. But what it all boils down to is the sonic rhythm that is created by putting the sound of certain words together in a particular order in each line.

When the words are sung, the syllables fall into rhythmic patterns in which some syllables are stressed and some are not. This creates an effect which sounds pleasant to the ears. The syllables that are emphasized tend to be longer, louder and have a higher pitch, whereas unstressed syllables are shorter.

The rhythmical effect comes from the way stressed and unstressed syllables bounce off each other. If we express a stressed syllable as 'DUM' and an unstressed syllable as 'dah', you can hear how the cadence changes when we go from 'dah-DUM, dah-DUM, dah-DUM, dah-DUM' to 'DUM-dah, DUM-dah, DUM-DUM-DUM'.

'Metric variation' is therefore the way in which the sound pattern is changed and made more interesting by selecting words that invert and vary the sequence of stressed and unstressed syllables.

Typical stressed/unstressed variations include: 'dah-DUM' or 'DUM-dah' or 'DUM-DUM' or 'dah-dah' (all two-syllable words), and 'dah-dah-DUM' or 'DUM-dah-dah' (three-syllable words), or 'dah-dah-DUM-dah' (four syllables). The syllables in a five-syllable word like 'unforgettable' would be expressed as 'dah-dah-DUM-dah-dah'. If you check your dictionary, you'll see how most multi-syllable words fit into one of these categories when you read them out loud.

Breaking a repeated 'dah-DUM' pattern simply by inserting a 'DUM-dah' line is a common method of metric variation.

Unlike poetry, the craft of writing lyrics involves matching the rhythmic sound patterns of syllables within each line to the patterns imposed by the beats and tempo of the music. The stressed syllables usually fall on the accented beats in a bar. A poor fit will make the song sound clumsy.

Because the verses, chorus and bridge all serve a different lyrical purpose, it is important to give each section a noticeably different meter and rhyming scheme—otherwise it will be difficult to reinforce the distinction between them. Listeners may not be able to tell where the verse ends and the chorus begins. This will make it much harder for your song to stand out.

Since verses are designed to tell the song's story, they usually have longer lines with less pronounced (or fewer) stresses.

The job of the chorus, meanwhile, is to hammer home the hook and the title line and make the song instantly memorable and singable. As a result, choruses tend to feature a meter that has shorter lyric lines and adheres more strictly to a repeating rhythmic pattern which helps to make the chorus stand out from the rest of the song.

These days, meter usually tries to simulate the rhythms of natural conversation rather than force lyrics into rigid, contrived forms. That's why almost all hit songs tend to have lyrics written in what is known as 'common meter'.

Common meter consists of four lyric lines like a nursery rhyme. Lines 1 and 3 typically have four stressed syllables (each preceded by an unstressed syllable), while Lines 2 and 4 only have three stressed syllables (also preceded by an unstressed syllable). The final syllable on Line 4 can sometimes be unstressed to signify the end of the section.

If we use 'DUM' and 'dah' again, common meter sounds like this:

Line 1: 'dah-DUM, dah-DUM, dah-DUM, dah-DUM'

Line 2: 'dah-DUM, dah-DUM, dah-DUM'

Line 3: 'dah-DUM, dah-DUM, dah-DUM, dah-DUM'

Line 4: 'dah-DUM, dah-DUM, dah-dah'.

The old folk song 'House of The Rising Sun' provides a typical example of common meter:

Line 1: There is a house in New Orleans

Line 2: They call the rising sun

Line 3: It's been the ruin of many poor boy

Line 4: And God, I know I'm one.

Common meter usually follows the ABAB rhyming scheme which means Lines 1 and 3 rhyme with each other, and Line 4 rhymes with Line 2 (although other rhyming patterns can also be used).

Metric variation is important because establishing a clear distinction between the structure of the verses, chorus and bridge can make a big difference to the overall feel, mood and emotional impact of a song. Variation can also be used for artistic effect, with more complex verbal rhythms sometimes used to heighten the dramatic tension (although this approach is rarely used in pure pop songs where simplicity is vital).

Variation can also be exploited stylistically by stretching out a word to form two or more syllables, the first of which is usually stressed. For example, the word 'good' is sung as "gu-oid" in Selena Gomez's 'Good For You', prolonging the vowel and making a simple word sound more interesting. Other examples include Lorde's song 'Royals' in which she breaks the one-syllable word 'care' into two syllables ("caye-aare"), and Katy Perry's 'Rise' in which 'story' is stretched to three syllables and sung as "story-yee".

Stretching vowels in this way can also be used to help the lyric fit the melody when a line requires more syllables than there are in the words you want to use. Certain vowels—such as 'i' (as in 'sigh') and 'ooh' (as in 'you')—lend themselves to being stretched.

Building plenty of variation into your metric structure—including different line lengths and different rhythmic patterns in consecutive lines—can help to hold listeners' attention. And if you incorporate one or two long lines (especially in the last line of the verse), you'll have more scope for internal rhymes which can add extra color and surprise the listener.

#34
INCONSISTENT USE OF TENSE

INEXPERIENCED WRITERS often fall into the trap of confusing listeners by not being consistent in their use of tense throughout a song—especially when the words in the chorus (which are usually the same in every chorus) don't hold up after the events described in a different tense in the preceding verse.

Remember, when people hear your song, they only know what you tell them in the lyrics—so it's vital to make sure the timeframe for a song is always clear, consistent and easy to follow.

This means all your lyrics should be in the same tense instead of time-traveling between past, present and future from line to line.

The consistent use of tense is important because it locates your song's story in a specific moment in time and helps listeners to understand when the action and the events described in the song take place.

If you start describing a situation that happened in the past, you shouldn't suddenly switch to talking about the same event as if it's taking place now. If the tense keeps changing, there is a danger that listeners will end up bewildered, and may simply lose interest in the song.

Getting the tense right can sometimes be a tricky business, though. Most people only think in terms of past, present or future. But, grammatically, lyricists are potentially faced with a multitude of different tenses— at least 12 of them, in fact.

For example, the **Simple Present Tense** is used to describe events, actions or situations that have started but haven't yet finished, although the lyric doesn't explain when they started or whether they're still active (for example, "I go to pieces over you…").

The **Present Progressive Tense** is about something that is happening right now ("I'm going to pieces over you…").

The **Present Perfect Tense** draws attention to the present consequences of a past event that has now finished, as opposed to describing when the event occurred ("I've gone to pieces over you…").

The **Present Perfect Progressive Tense** is used for an ongoing action in the past which continues right up to the present (or has recently finished), although the lyric doesn't explain when it started ("I've been going to pieces over you…").

The **Simple Past Tense** recounts events or actions that happened at some point in the past and are now completed ("I went to pieces over you…").

The **Past Progressive Tense** is used to describe events that were happening at a point in the past but are being talked about at this moment, and may still be happening currently ("I was going to pieces over you…").

The **Past Perfect Tense** portrays situations that had already been completed at the specific point in time that you're writing about ("I had gone to pieces over you…").

The **Past Perfect Progressive Tense** is similar to the Present Perfect Progressive, except the point in time referred to in the lyric is in the past ("I had been going to pieces over you…").

And there are many more different tenses with definitions that will make your brain ache!!

The key, though, is to define your time frame upfront and decide which tense you intend to use in a new song—and then stick to it.

As you write more songs, you'll start to develop an instinct for choosing the most appropriate tense for each lyric.

The past tense is usually ideal for story songs that have a clear flow of time. The present tense is often best for love songs or songs with a strong emotional message because it can add a sense of immediacy to the story. According to one study, more than 80% of up-tempo hits are set in the present.

While the most effective lyrics tend to stay in one tense, it doesn't mean the event flow within your song has to be linear.

For example, you can use devices such as flashbacks as long as you include a transitioning word or phrase such as "I remember when…" or "Last night…". This 'linking' phrase shows the connection between past and present and explains the change of tense to the listener.

It's quite common for hit songwriters to show how past events have impacted on a current situation by putting the first two verses in the past tense and switching to the present in the chorus and final verse. For example, saying "I was going to pieces over you" in the verse, but in the chorus proclaiming: "I'm over you now and my life is full of sunshine".

In addition, there is often scope for changing tense in the bridge to provide a 'release' from the rest of the song.

In general, though, it's best to avoid changing tense unless it is essential to your story. The tense that you choose for your lyrics can significantly affect the way your song connects with listeners.

When you've finished writing your lyrics, always check to confirm that the timeframe or flow of time is consistent throughout the song.

And, as an extra safeguard, make sure you haven't unknowingly changed tense in places where you didn't intend to.

# # # #

#35

NOT LETTING THE LYRIC MOVE FORWARD

*"I write a song from beginning to end.
I don't go in sections. It's a story."*
—Adele

BE CAREFUL not to fall into the common trap of writing a great first line and then, without realizing it, simply restating that line in different ways throughout the rest of the song.

A song needs to develop and progress in order to hold the listener's interest.

That's why every word in every subsequent line should be carefully chosen to move the song forward in a logical sequence, rather than merely creating nice word pictures that don't actually lead anywhere.

Some professional writers find it helpful to sketch out the complete storyline for a new song in a few paragraphs of prose, just like a short story or a mini 'treatment' for a movie or a novel.

They then add rhymes to the prose and turn the words used in the 'treatment' into the song's lyrics.

You may also find it helpful to approach each new verse as if you were a screenwriter creating a sequence of movie scenes.

You can build on the central storyline of your 'movie' by focusing on a specific scenario in each verse so that it ties in with the previous 'scene' and the one that follows it. Adding new and relevant information in each line of every verse in this way is essential to progressing the story.

In other words, the second verse and third verse (if there is one) should not just say the same thing that you said in the first verse.

After establishing the setting in the first verse, you must then tell the listener what happened next, or provide more information about the central characters in the song, or expand on your description of the singer's state of mind.

"Generally I start from the top, first line, first verse, and go all the way through the song," explained the late, great American lyricist Linda Creed (co-writer of classic songs such as 'The Greatest Love of All', 'Stop, Look, Listen (To Your Heart)' and 'I'm Stone in Love with You'. "I can't go to another line unless I have the line before it completed."

She added: "A lot of people write lyrics and there's a line in there that's a really great, heavy line, but you say 'What the hell are they talking about?' because it has nothing to do with what they said before. To me, if you're going to state something, state it so that it's understandable. I believe in proper English, in completed thoughts, completed sentences."

Hal David always warned new writers to be careful not to lose sight of their original inspiration for the song as the lyric moves forward.

"Every writer sets out to achieve something with their lyrics," said David, "but various things can conspire against you during the writing process to make you lose sight of the initial emotional intent."

One way to make sure your lyrics have an easy-to-understand linear flow is to look at the overall picture of the song and produce a 'map' of your lyrics.

Start by writing down a phrase or a sentence that sums up the main idea of the song and your emotional goal.

Then create a simple flowchart on a piece of paper by drawing a separate box for each different section of the song, with an arrow leading to the next section.

For example:

Verse One > Chorus > Verse Two > Chorus > Verse Three > Chorus > Bridge > Chorus.

In each box, insert a phrase that summarizes the main point that you want to convey lyrically in that section.

The lyrics should be the same in every chorus; so only the words in the verses and the bridge need to change as the story moves forward.

If you find you're struggling to come up with something new to say in the second and third verses, don't worry. You're not alone. Even top songwriters often find the lyrics for the second verse are the hardest to write. They call it "second verse hell".

However, experienced writers have a simple way of overcoming this block ...

If they've completed the lyrics for their first verse and chorus—and there seems to be nowhere else to go because everything they wanted to say has already been said—they simply make the first verse their second verse.

This means they have to come up with another first verse!

After you've written the first verse, subsequent verses and the bridge should go deeper into the storyline—just like a tale unfolding in each new chapter of a novel. Unlike a novel, though, you only have about three minutes and a limited number of words to really explore your theme.

"If you have a clear idea of what you want to say," observed American country singer-songwriter Lyle Lovett, "then you know when you have said it, and the song is finished."

# # # #

#36

YOUR RHYMES ARE TOO PREDICTABLE

"The ears expect certain rhymes, so you want to fool them because one of the things you want to do in a song is surprise an audience"
—Stephen Sondheim

AS A PUBLISHER I have often listened to demos by aspiring songwriters and, despite always hoping to discover a fresh new talent, ended up feeling disappointed because I found that I could predict what the next rhyme was going to be on almost every line.

Inexperienced writers often weaken a potentially good song by going for the easiest and most obvious rhyme, or by using the same rhyme sound too many times in a row.

This simply makes the lyrics sound boring, monotonous and colorless.

It's not enough to simply go through the alphabet looking for words that rhyme, irrespective of whether or not the chosen word helps to underpin the meaning of your song and drive the story forward.

This lazy approach usually results in worn-out, clichéd rhymes that we've all heard countless times before.

These days, you have to be more creatively adventurous. So challenge yourself and make your rhymes less predictable.

Surprise the listener.

Lyrics don't always have to rhyme, of course, but rhyming is a mnemonic device that assists the memory and makes it easier for people to remember a song. Rhyming also plays an important part in giving a lyric a sense of form and symmetry.

James Fenton—a former Professor of Poetry at Oxford University—considers a rhyme to be a kind of "marker" for the end of a line.

"In a couplet, the first rhyme is like a question to which the second rhyme is an answer," he explains. "In most quatrains [four-line verses], space is created between the rhyme that poses the question and the rhyme that gives the answer ... it's like a pleasure deferred."

Historically, many pop songs in the rock era have featured 'perfect' rhymes where a one-syllable word is rhymed with another one-syllable word (such as 'kiss' and 'miss'), or where two words have the same spelling in the last syllable (such as 'love and 'above').

But many of these perfect rhymes have been used so many times over the years that they have now become clichés.

Hit songwriting is more sophisticated these days, and publishers and A&R reps have much higher expectations of lyricists.

If you have a rhyme in your head, ask yourself if you've heard it before. If it sounds familiar, try finding another way of saying it—perhaps by using a metaphor rather than just a literal rhyme.

Sometimes, simply putting an unexpected adjective or a visual descriptor (like Homer's "rosy-fingered dawn" and "wine-dark sea") in front of a clichéd rhyming noun can surprise the listener and make the cliché sound less familiar.

You can often create a much greater impact by rhyming words that don't have the same combination of letters but sound similar (such as 'clown' and 'around', or 'made' and 'late').

In fact, sound-alike words tend to engage listeners more than words with the same spelling. This is because lyrics are meant for the ears, so how words sound is more important than how they're written. It's the similarity between the sound of the syllables that creates the rhyme, not the words themselves.

"Rhyming doesn't have to be exact anymore," Bob Dylan told Paul Zollo of *American Songwriter* magazine in a 2012 interview. "It gives you a thrill to rhyme something and you think, 'Well, that's never been rhymed before'. Nobody's going to care if you rhyme 'represent' with 'ferment', you know. Nobody's gonna care."

Dylan once admitted to *Rolling Stone* magazine that he stunned himself when he wrote the first two lines of 'Like a Rolling Stone' and rhymed "kiddin' you" with "didn't you".

"It just about knocked me out," he said.

In fact, many established songwriters now try to steer clear of perfect rhymes because, they say, rhymes that are too exact can limit the expression of true emotion. Using 'false' rhymes to create word pictures—or to convey what you want to say more accurately—can often be much more effective than pure rhymes.

With false rhymes (also referred to as imperfect rhymes, half rhymes, slant rhymes or near-rhymes), the vowel sounds are identical, but the consonants that follow or precede those vowel sounds are different and don't match. For example: 'forever' and 'together', 'time' and 'mind', or 'make' and 'fate'. The matching vowels are enough to make the rhyme work.

Many experienced writers feel that using imperfect rhymes gives them greater freedom and flexibility to create word pictures. It also provides an ingenious way to avoid employing rhyming clichés or rhymes that are too obvious.

For example, in her award-winning 2013 song 'Brave' (co-written with Jack Antonoff), Sara Bareilles rhymes 'outcast' with 'backlash', 'inside' with 'sunlight', 'there' with 'stared' and 'run' with 'tongue'.

Imperfect rhymes have always been used in hip hop in conjunction with assonance (the repetition of vowel sounds to create internal rhyming within lyric lines). For example, in one section of his 1992 song 'N.Y. State of Mind', rapper Nas manages to rhyme the word 'prosperous' with 'dangerous', 'blamin' us' and 'hostages'.

Unpredictable rhymes can also be created by varying the rhyme sounds in your choice of words. For example, a single-sound rhyme in a multi-syllable word (such as 'indicate' and 'celebrate' or 'fingernail' and 'fairy tale'), You can also use double-sound rhymes ('walking' and 'talking'), or triple-sound rhymes ('addiction' and 'prediction').

Instead of rhyming a noun with a noun, or a verb with a verb, you can also create an unexpected rhyme by pairing different parts of speech—such as a noun and an adjective (for example, 'guess' and 'pointless').

When it comes to being less predictable, it's okay to use a rhyming dictionary for inspiration. Stephen Sondheim does it. So does Eminem. In fact, most top songwriters admit they always keep a rhyming dictionary and a thesaurus handy.

So don't feel it will make you any less creative. It will actually make you *more* adventurous and give you many more options—including multi-syllable rhyme words that you might not otherwise have thought of.

Even when you're using a rhyming dictionary, don't always go for the most obvious rhyme word. By digging deeper, and maybe cross-referencing with a book of synonyms, you can often discover rhymes that inspire new themes or fresh ideas that can take your lyrics in a more exciting (and less predictable) direction.

# # # #

#37

NOT VARYING YOUR RHYME PATTERNS

ONE OF the most common traps that new writers fall into is placing their rhymes in exactly the same position in the chorus as in the verses.

By not varying the rhyme pattern in the song's journey from the verse to the chorus, they fail to build the energy and momentum required to prepare listeners for the all-important hook in the chorus.

Experienced writers use rhyme as a strategy for attracting and holding the listener's attention.

They deliberately vary the rhyming pattern (also known as the 'rhyme scheme') in the verse, chorus and bridge so that each section sounds different and has its own personality.

Changing the placement of the rhymes and the rhythm of the lyric in the chorus can also help to reinforce the change in melody that takes place—and so give the chorus a unique shape that really makes it stand out.

The most common rhyme pattern in a four-line verse has traditionally involved making the first line rhyme with the third line, while the second and fourth lines also rhyme (this is known as an ABAB rhyme scheme).

These days, however, verses are just as likely to follow an AXXA or XAXA scheme, where the 'X' lines don't rhyme with each other or with any other line. Only the 'A' lines rhyme.

This kind of loose rhyming pattern allows greater creative freedom because you can use the two non-rhyming ('X') lines to develop the song's story without having to worry about finding words that rhyme. It also allows you to use a more conversational lyrical style.

You can add a little extra tension to a four-line verse by using an AXAA, or AAXA pattern (where only the 'A' lines rhyme with each other). The 'X' line (the non-rhyming line) is left hanging. This can subconsciously take listeners by surprise because their ears expect to hear a rhyme.

In today's more conversational verse lyrics, you can also surprise listeners by inserting imperfect or 'near' rhymes in your rhyming pattern instead of always using perfect rhymes.

When people hear the word 'man', for example, they will naturally expect to hear something like 'can' or 'ran' as the rhyme. If you unexpectedly slip in a rhyme that has an extra consonant at the end (for example, the word 'stand'), they may listen more closely to hear what comes next.

Pairing a word like 'man' with 'stand,' or 'soul' with 'gold', is known as an augmented rhyme because of the extra consonant at the end of the rhyming word.

An augmented rhyme is usually more satisfying to the ear than using the shorter word (without the consonant) as the rhyming mate. For example, 'stand' then 'man' as the rhyme, or 'gold' then 'soul'.

Putting the shorter word second is known as a diminished rhyme.

If you study the latest chart hits and compare where the rhymes are positioned, and what kind of rhymes are being used, you're likely to find much looser (and more conversational) 'near rhymes' placed in the middle of the lines in the verse, instead of at the end of each line (which is the traditional approach).

An internal rhyming pattern involves repeating vowels and consonants (and combinations of both) within each individual line. A good example of this is Phil Lynott's classic Thin Lizzy song 'With Love' which includes the line: "I must confess that in my quest I felt depressed and restless".

Using internal or 'mid-line' rhymes in this way helps to build the lyrical rhythm and can strengthen the forward motion of the verse.

You can also surprise listeners by having your internal rhyme fall on the second or third syllable of a multi-syllable word instead of at the end—for example, by putting the rhyme on the syllable that is stressed most strongly in normal speech (such as 'unach_iev_able' and 'bel_iev_able').

You can also rhyme a multi-syllable word with a word that only has one syllable (such as 'sublime' and 'time').

Eminem tends to fill his songs with more internal rhymes than anyone else in contemporary pop. He once told *Rolling Stone* magazine: "Even as a kid, I always wanted the most words to rhyme. Say I saw a word like 'transcendalistic tendencies'. I would write it out on a piece of paper and underneath I'd line a word up with each syllable. Even if it didn't make sense, that's the kind of drill I would do."

But remember, you have to be consistent. If you use internal rhymes in the first verse, you should try to put them in the same place in the subsequent verses as well to maintain the kind of symmetry that listeners like to hear.

While verses have shifted towards less rigid rhyming patterns, choruses have moved in the opposite direction.

In many hit songs there is now a greater emphasis on tight rhyming couplets at the end of each line in the chorus—like the ABAB pattern mentioned earlier.

Some high-impact choruses also use an AABB scheme (where the first and second lines rhyme, as do the third and fourth lines) ... or an ABCB scheme (where only the second and fourth lines rhyme) ... or an ABBA pattern (where the first and fourth lines rhyme with each other, and the second and third lines also rhyme).

You can also establish a clear difference between the verses and the chorus by varying the primary vowel sounds in each rhyme in the chorus—so that some rhyme lines end with long vowels and others have shorter vowel sounds.

This clear contrast between the loose rhyme pattern in the verses and the tighter end-of-the-line rhymes in the chorus can have a significant impact on listeners and their ability to remember the song.

But don't forget, the rhyming pattern that you choose for the verse should be the same in every verse even though the words are different—whereas the words and the rhyme scheme in the chorus should *remain the same* whenever the chorus is repeated.

This enables you to really hammer home the hook and the title line.

# # # #

#38

NOT CHECKING SINGABILITY

"You can say things a million times, but if you can't sing it, then it really isn't much of a song."
—Justin Timberlake

INEXPERIENCED LYRICISTS who aren't singers—or poets who are trying their hand at writing lyrics—often don't realize the importance of 'singability'.

They don't fully appreciate that artists need to be able to sing the words comfortably, and the cadences of the lyric should leave subtle breathing spaces for the singer.

Remember, as a lyricist you're writing words to be sung not read ... and some words are easier to sing than others.

Your song is not going to be picked up if you've written a great set of creative and emotive lyrics that look amazing on the page but later prove to be too difficult or awkward for an artist to sing.

This was an important lesson learned by Michael Chabon—the acclaimed American author—when he was asked to write lyrics for more than half the tracks on Mark Ronson's 2015 album, *Uptown Special*. Chabon admitted that adapting the relative freedom of his novel-writing style to the precise musical and rhythmic restrictions of a song was a challenge.

When he first started working on the tracks, Chabon found that his lines were much too long with far too many syllables. "There was this whole issue of singability I had no experience of," Chabon told *The Guardian* newspaper.

In order to take singability into consideration, writers need to understand that a singer's mouth has to continually re-shape itself to be able to sing certain vowels and consonants in a sequence.

How hard the lips, tongue and teeth have to work depends on how particular words (especially three- or four-syllable words) are strung together over a musical phrase.

Sammy Cahn always gave this advice to new writers: "Go over and over the lyric. Sing it until no word sticks in the mouth. Be sure every word, every phrase, every syllable sings effortlessly."

For your song to have an emotional impact on an audience, the singer needs to be able to deliver the words as convincingly as he or she would say them in real life. If a singer has to use unnatural-sounding pronunciations just to make the words fit with the notes, it can jar with listeners.

The general rule is: 'If you can't say it that way in normal conversation, you can't sing it that way'.

Writing 'like people speak' means constructing a lyric line in a way that still preserves the natural shape of the words when you're matching stressed syllables with the emphasized notes or beats in the melody. If your words aren't placed on the right notes, they won't sing. For example, it's much easier for singers if the first or last syllable of a multi-syllable word sits on an accented note.

As mentioned earlier in this book, the skillful use of lyric meter also allows writers to emphasize natural speech patterns in their lyrics while linking them to the melody and the rhythm of the music.

This helps to ensure that the words fit comfortably with the tune without putting the accents on the wrong syllables or trying to squeeze too many words into too little musical space.

Experienced writers know it's much harder for artists to sing a song (and remember the words) if stressed syllables and emphasized notes don't complement each other. Singers can get confused because part of their brain is trying to follow the melody and sing it correctly, while another part of their brain is instinctively trying to say the words normally.

Words that have long vowel sounds are much easier to sing, which is why professional writers tend to use a lot of open vowels such as 'a', 'e', 'i', 'o' and 'oo'. These sounds enable singers to hold the all-important word at the end of a line more easily.

Pros also try to use words that contain the most singable consonants.

The liquid consonants 'l' and 'r' (as in 'led' and 'red') and the nasal consonants 'm', 'n' and 'ng' (as in 'mouth', 'nose' and 'danc<u>ing</u>') are the easiest to sing.

Other key points to remember include:

—Single syllable words make a song much easier to sing.

—Accented syllables should fall on the accented notes of the melody.

—Vowels are far easier to sing and hold than consonants.

—Too many sibilants ('s', 'z', 'sh', 'ch') can cause problems, especially at the end of a word.

—Some word sounds are harder to sing at the upper or lower end of a singer's vocal range.

—Words should ideally end with sounds that open the singer's mouth, not close it.

Good breath management skills are essential for singers if they want to sound great and maintain the quality of their vocal performance every time. But if you put too many words in your lyrics and don't allow the singer enough space to breathe, it can have a negative impact on his or her vocal quality—and your song may be rejected as a result.

That's why it's important to structure phrases in such a way that the singer can take a breath without it sounding awkward (just like breathing naturally between sentences when you're talking).

Words on notes held for more than a few beats should ideally be followed by a rest long enough to allow a breath.

You should also leave some breathing space after phrases, or multi-syllable words, which sit on a sequence of fast, short notes.

The best way to check the 'breathability' of your lyrics is to read them out loud against a metronome or a click track, and mark all of the points at which you find yourself taking a breath in normal speech.

The next step is to make sure the words you're asking the vocalist to sing correspond with these natural pauses.

As Stephen Sondheim once observed: "One of the hardest things about writing lyrics is to make the lyrics sit on the music in such a way that you're not aware there was a writer there,"

It's also essential to leave enough spaces to allow artists to express themselves and interpret the song in their own way.

One simple method of creating spaces is to remove any unnecessary coordinating conjunctions such as 'for', 'and', 'nor', 'but', 'because', 'or', 'yet', and 'so'.

Sprinkling clever alliteration, assonance and consonance into your songs can add extra interest to your lyrics. But always keep the singer in mind and use these creative devices selectively. New writers sometimes tend to over-do clever wordplay—resulting in lyrics that may be hard to sing because they contain too many 'tongue twisters'.

As James Fenton, a former Professor of Poetry at Oxford University, explains: "One thing you have to pay particular attention to with songwriting is not to write unintentional tongue twisters. A song has to flow off the tongue … You must be very kind to the singer."

Another form of unintentional tongue twister can occur with adjoining words—for example, when you begin a new word with the same sound as the consonant sound at the end of the previous word (such as 'ri*ch ch*ick' or 'stran*ge g*eneration'). You have to allow enough space between the words to allow the poor singer's tongue to recover.

If you're writing the lyrics first—rather than coming up with words to fit an existing melody—the best way to make sure your lyrics will sing well is to sing them to a dummy tune as you write them. If you're not a singer, read the lyrics out loud rhythmically, ideally at the tempo at which they are likely to be performed.

If the words feel awkward and don't flow well, you'll have to find easier ways to say the same thing.

If you consistently scan your lyrics in this way, they are more likely to pass the singability test.

A final word of warning. Listen carefully to how your words rub together. Check for any adjoining words that risk being delivered by a singer in such a way that they could be misheard and misunderstood by listeners. The classic example of this is Jimi Hendrix's 1967 song 'Purple Haze' which includes the line: "scuse me while I kiss the sky". Many people misheard it as "scuse me while I kiss this guy".

In 2016, a survey in the UK found that many recent hit songs have suffered the same fate. Misheard tracks included Selina Gomez's 2015 hit, 'Good For You'. In the first verse, Selina's breathy voice sings the line: "I'm fourteen carats". But many listeners embarrassingly heard it as: "I'm farting carrots" …

# # # #

#39

NOT USING ENOUGH POLISH

"One thing a lyricist must learn is not to fall in love with his own lines. Once you learn that, you can walk away from the lyric and look at it with a reasonable degree of objectivity."
—Hal David

ONE OF the biggest mistakes that developing writers make is to think their latest lyrics are finished as soon as they've found a rhyme for the last line. The first draft could, of course, prove to be the one and the song may indeed be ready for the demo studio. But in the majority of cases, 'finishing' a lyric is just the beginning.

Your aim should be to write extraordinary lyrics—not just settle for good ones.

So it's time to start polishing your new creation to make it shine even brighter.

Professional songwriters know that every new song they write will probably need several re-writes before they have the final version. They've learned that creating a great lyric usually requires 10% writing and 90% re-writing.

"Often the process of 'neatening up' that one troublesome rhyme can be more time-consuming than writing the entire piece," lyricist Sammy Cahn once remarked.

However, you should never allow yourself to be discouraged by the amount of re-writing and editing that may be necessary in order to bring your lyrics up to the high standard that music publishers, A&R execs and producers (and artists themselves) now expect.

Look on it as simply part of the overall songwriting process.

As the producer and composer Quincy Jones observed: "The best songwriters are re-writers."

Pro writers often produce a first draft of a new lyric, then put it down for a few days and listen to it again later. That's usually when they can tell if the lyric truly has potential.

Listening to it from a fresh perspective enables them to spot any weaknesses and assess how the lyrics can be improved.

The legendary lyricist Johnny Mercer always gave this advice to new writers: "Don't try to do too much too quickly.

He explained: "You write a number, and even if you think it's great, put it away, let it cook, let it simmer …

"Then you come back to it, and you may have a different slant. You play with it, fix it, let it grow."

One of the purposes of this book is to give you a detailed checklist that you can measure your lyrics against, no matter how finished you think they are.

The aim is to help you improve each new song by making sure you haven't made any fundamental mistakes at each key stage in the development of your lyrics.

So don't make the mistake of shying away from the tough decisions that often have to be made at the re-writing stage—especially if strengthening a lyric means having to change or leave out some of your favorite words, rhymes, or even complete verses that you started out with.

You have to be brutal and take a pair of scissors to any lines that you realize are average, banal or clichéd (and therefore aren't likely to impress anyone).

Sometimes the best editing is done when you remove unnecessary words. It results in a shorter text, but leaves something much clearer and more concise.

"I try to be as economic as possible in my language and be as specific as I can be in the words," country singer-songwriter Mary Chapin Carpenter told *Acoustic Guitar* magazine in 2016.

"I write on a yellow legal pad with a pencil and eraser," she said, "and I just edit, edit, edit, edit, edit, with the guitar in my lap. I want it to feel like that is the word that belongs there and there's no fluff."

Editing and re-writing can be hard work. However, it's an essential step if you want your lyrics to succeed.

American rapper and songwriter Nicki Minaj says she often re-writes her verses up to 10 times because she wants them to be perfect.

Re-writing may require finding a fresh way of saying what you want to say, or correcting some of the common mistakes highlighted in this book.

At the same time, though, you have to polish your work without losing the spontaneity and spark of inspiration that gave you the idea for the lyric in the first place.

So it's better to take your time and keep reworking every line until it sounds exceptional. You'll feel the magic happening as the right words and phrases finally fall into place.

"I spend inordinate amounts of time deciding whether 'and' or 'but' is the right word," said Hal David. "To a certain extent, lyrics flow easily, but no matter how much they flow at a given time, by the time you get it together, finished and refined to the best of your ability, it's a lot of work."

You have to be ruthlessly honest with yourself. If you feel the lyric is the absolute best you can do, then go ahead and submit the song.

But if you have the slightest doubt, you must be prepared to focus on identifying the weaknesses in the lyrics—and fix them—before spending time and money on making a demo, or showing the song to your collaborator (if you have one).

If you're a singer-songwriter, or write songs for your own band, a lyric that is 'close enough' for performing on stage won't be good enough for publishers, A&R managers and producers. They have to operate in the tough commercial world of the music business … which means they'll be tough on your songs too.

If you've ever had to endure the agony of having songs rejected by a publisher or a record company, now is the time to ask yourself:

'Could I have made the songs better if I'd spent more time polishing them?'.

Writers who aren't willing to re-visit or re-work their lyrics may find that those painful rejection slips will continue to pile up in the letter-box …

# # # #

#40

THE LYRICS AREN'T CLEAR ON YOUR DEMO

IF YOUR ambition is to earn money from writing songs, it's important to remember that a demo is more than just a permanent recording of your creative endeavors for posterity.

A demo is the advertisement for your song.

It's your most important marketing tool.

Like any advertisement you see on TV or in a magazine, your demo has to be able to attract people's attention and stimulate their interest. Most importantly, it has to help you *sell* the song.

So it's crucial to spend time getting the demo right.

Have you ever seen an advertisement that simply displays a picture of a product and doesn't include any words that explain what the product is called or what it does? In the case of a brand new product that nobody has ever heard of, such a vague ad would probably result in zero sales.

Similarly, a demo is like an advertisement for a new song that nobody has ever heard before. So the same criteria apply. People need *words* to tell them the title and what the song is all about so they can decide whether or not to buy it.

This means a demo has to sell your lyrics as well as the music—so it's essential for the lead vocal to be upfront in the mix to make sure listeners can hear the words clearly.

Getting a hot mix is a critical part of producing a professional-sounding recording. But all you need on a good demo is a solid, tight rhythm track with a strong lead vocal that stays in tune. The music should never be allowed to drown out the singer ... or the lyrics.

And don't be tempted to use too much auto-tune. It can be extremely distracting on a demo. All you need is an audio mix with a clear vocal that will allow A&R execs to hear your lyrics in their full glory.

Bear in mind that the people you submit your demo to aren't likely to listen to the track for the first time on studio-quality speakers. Most of the publishers, A&R people and producers that I know usually listen to new demos in the car, on a laptop or a mobile device while commuting, or on a small audio system in their office.

So it's always best to mix your demo down to small speakers ... and make sure the lyrics are still intelligible at that level of sound quality.

In fact, with more music industry pros listening to demos on headphones or earbuds, it could be a good idea to do your mixing on headphones, especially if you record your demos in your own home studio. Mixing on headphones is becoming more and more prevalent in the pro audio world too and is therefore a legitimate way for you to guarantee that people will hear exactly what you want them to hear.

And remember, if someone is listening to your demo while travelling, they may not have a copy of the lyrics with them. So that's another reason to make sure the vocal and the lyrics are crystal clear.

If publishers, A&R reps and producers have to strain to pick out the words, they may just hit the 'stop' button … and move on to someone else's demo.

# # # #

CHECKLIST

—Are you keeping your 'writer's antenna' switched on at all times so you can cultivate a constant stream of lyric ideas from the world around you?

—Are you carrying a notebook, or using the voice-memo app on your phone, to capture great ideas whenever you spot them (so you won't let them get away)?

—Are you keeping a list of 'ready-made' ideas (titles and phrases) that you can dip into?

—Have you identified the most creative time of day for you to write?

—Have you chosen a special writing place where you can focus and be creative?

—Have you established a daily writing routine and are you sticking to it? Are you writing something every day?

—Have you set yourself daily, weekly and monthly objectives and deadlines?

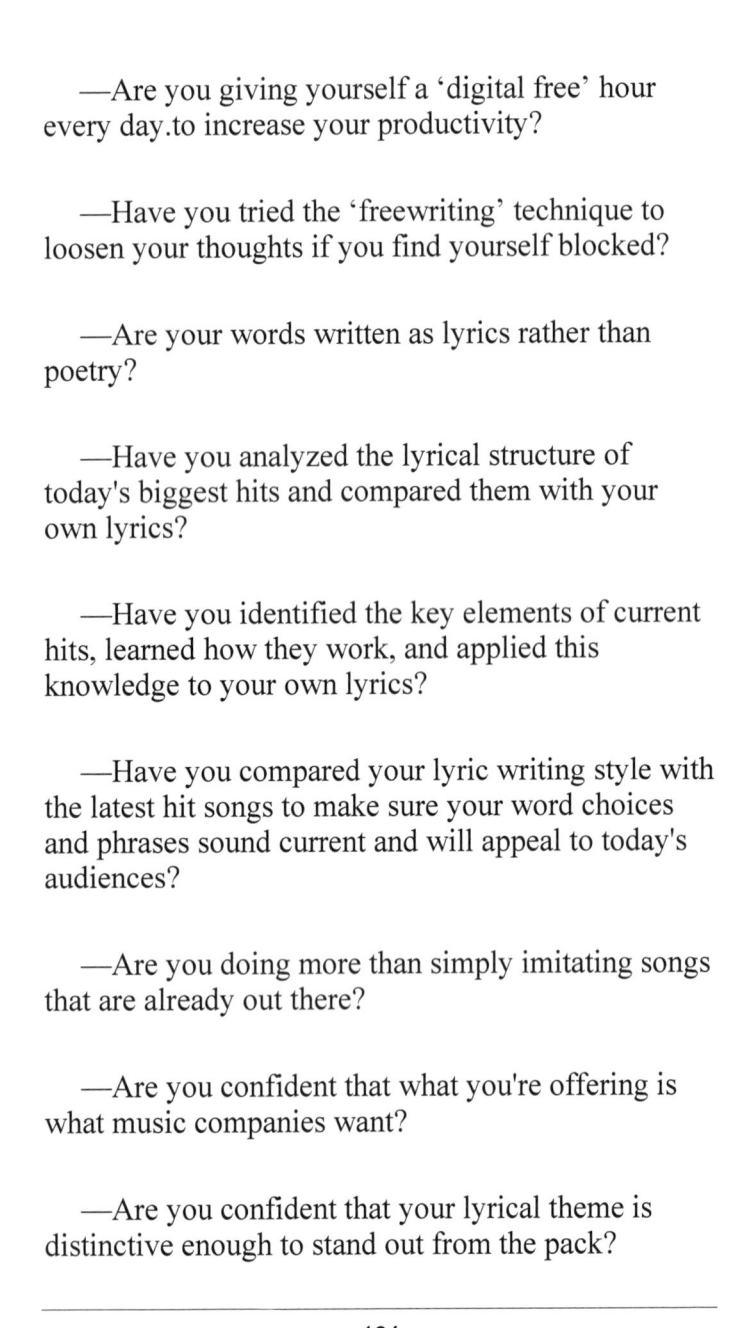

—Are you giving yourself a 'digital free' hour every day.to increase your productivity?

—Have you tried the 'freewriting' technique to loosen your thoughts if you find yourself blocked?

—Are your words written as lyrics rather than poetry?

—Have you analyzed the lyrical structure of today's biggest hits and compared them with your own lyrics?

—Have you identified the key elements of current hits, learned how they work, and applied this knowledge to your own lyrics?

—Have you compared your lyric writing style with the latest hit songs to make sure your word choices and phrases sound current and will appeal to today's audiences?

—Are you doing more than simply imitating songs that are already out there?

—Are you confident that what you're offering is what music companies want?

—Are you confident that your lyrical theme is distinctive enough to stand out from the pack?

—If you're writing lyrics to someone else's melody, did you listen closely what the melody was saying before you started on the words?

—Are your lyrics built on the mood and emotional foundations laid down by the melody?

—Do your words and the melody sound like they belong together?

—If you're writing a love song, is it a sad one?

—Have you structured your lyrics to reflect the important variance between the verse, pre-chorus, chorus and bridge which each have very different responsibilities?

—Are you confident that your song title is distinctive, intriguing and memorable enough to attract people's interest and so help you sell the song?

—Will your title make an effective promotional hashtag for social media?

—Have you positioned the title in the right place within the lyrics?

—Does your title tell listeners what the song is about in just one word or a short phrase?

—Is the title simple, catchy and straight to the point?

—Have you built your lyrics from the central idea contained in the title?

—Have you placed the title line in the strongest possible position within your lyrics, such as on the first or last line of your chorus?

—Have you tried to make your opening line memorable and engaging, so it will draw listeners into the song and keep them listening?

—Do your lyrics in the verses move the story forward rather than simply restate what has already been said?

—Is the story clear and easy to follow?

—Have you given your lyrics a killer high point and put it in the right place within the song?

—Apart from the title line, have you given your lyrics an instantly memorable lyrical hook that will immediately grab listeners' attention and stick in their mind?

—Have you placed the lyrical hook in the important final line of the chorus?

—Do your lyrics get to the first chorus and the hook in less than 60 seconds?

—Have you avoided forcing the development of your lyric and allowed it to come to life in its own time?

—If your song is for an established artist, have you fully researched the artist's style and background to make sure your lyrics are appropriate?

—Are your lyrics written with the listener in mind?

—Will other people be able to relate to your words? Or are they too personal or self-indulgent?

—Were you clear about the whole point of the song before you started writing the lyrics?

—Have you made sure your lyrics are clearly focused on making only one major point from one point of view?

—Have you checked to make sure you've used pronouns consistently so that each character is represented by the same pronoun every time?

—Have you made sure the story is told from the same point of view throughout the lyrics?

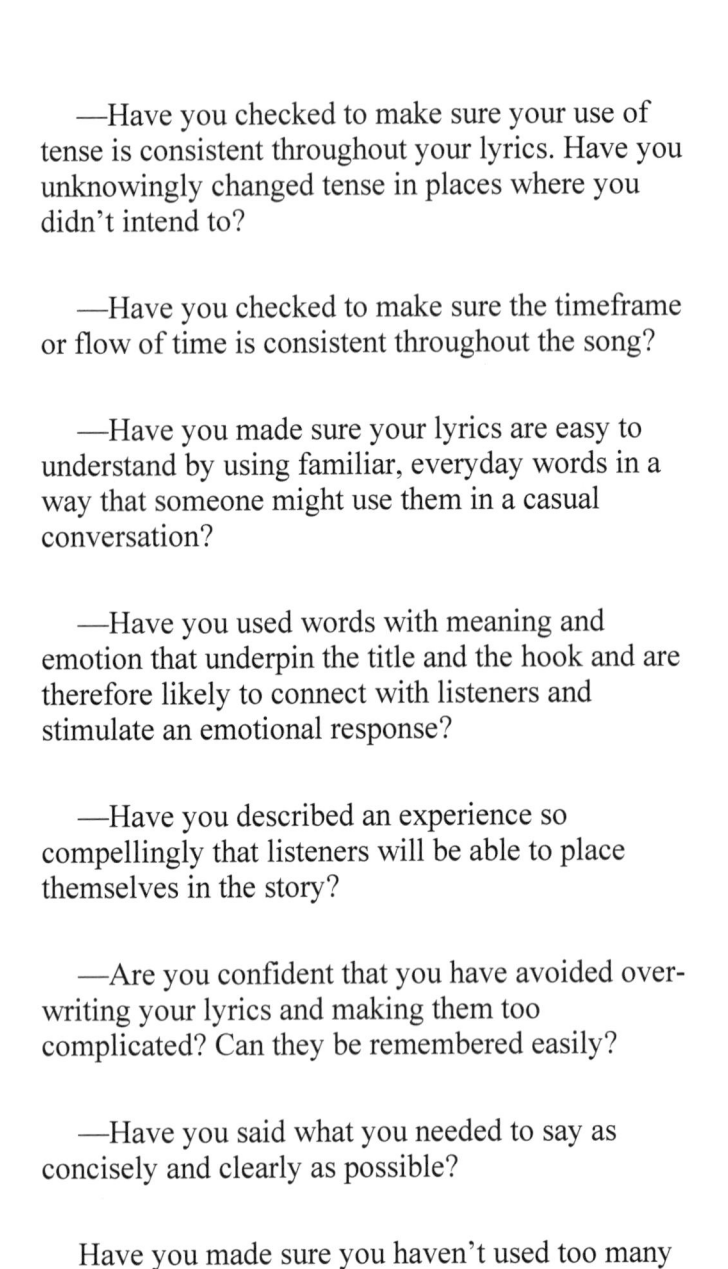

—Have you checked to make sure your use of tense is consistent throughout your lyrics. Have you unknowingly changed tense in places where you didn't intend to?

—Have you checked to make sure the timeframe or flow of time is consistent throughout the song?

—Have you made sure your lyrics are easy to understand by using familiar, everyday words in a way that someone might use them in a casual conversation?

—Have you used words with meaning and emotion that underpin the title and the hook and are therefore likely to connect with listeners and stimulate an emotional response?

—Have you described an experience so compellingly that listeners will be able to place themselves in the story?

—Are you confident that you have avoided over-writing your lyrics and making them too complicated? Can they be remembered easily?

—Have you said what you needed to say as concisely and clearly as possible?

Have you made sure you haven't used too many words and made your lyric lines too crowded?

—Whether your song is a first-person or third-person lyric, have you fully developed the central character and given listeners a clear picture of who he or she is?

—Is your central character distinctive and believable, so listeners can easily visualize and identify with her or him?

—Have you made sure you haven't written too many verses? (two or three high-impact verses should be sufficient)?

—Have you concentrated on conveying just one strong message or emotion and built your song around it, while being creative but concise in your phrasing?

—Is the structure of your lyric familiar enough so that listeners will feel comfortable with it, without it being too predictable?

—Have you made sure your key words and phrases are repeated often enough to emphasize important information and make the song sound instantly memorable?

—Are the words in the repeated sections (especially in the chorus) exactly the same each time they appear?

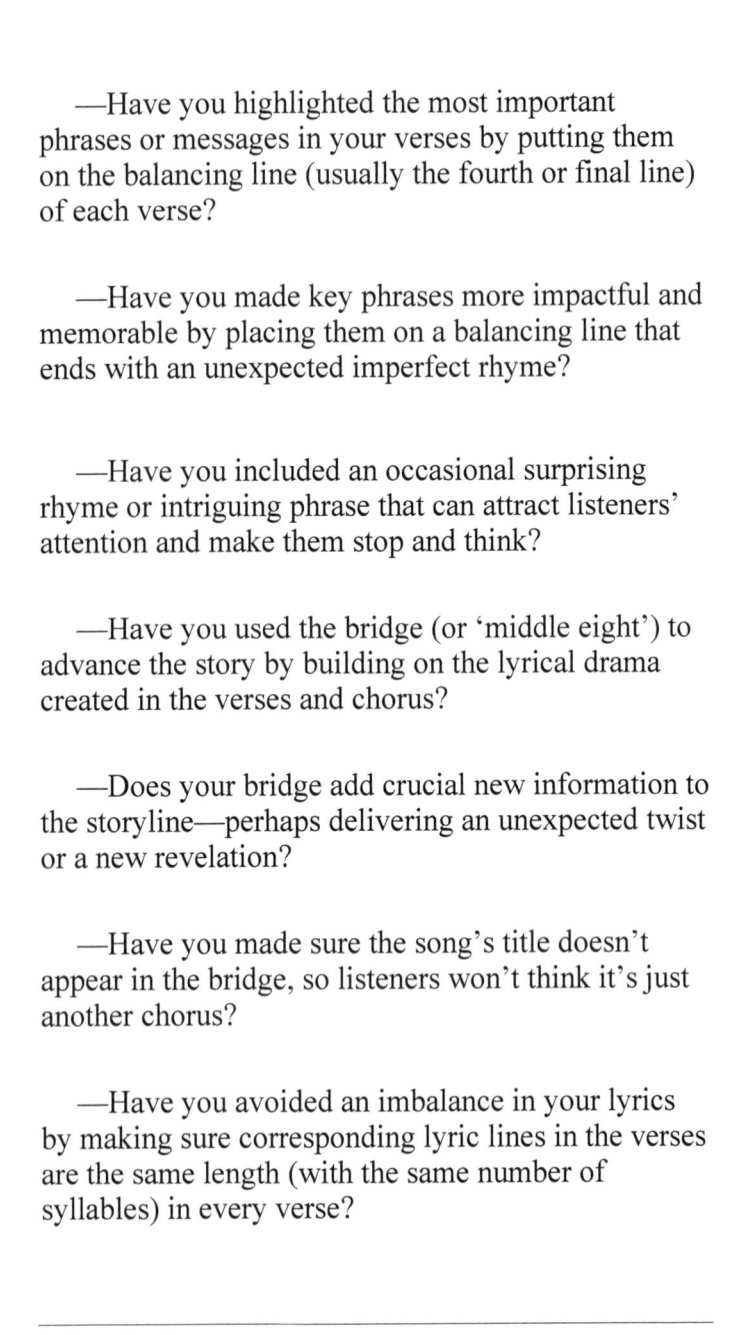

—Have you highlighted the most important phrases or messages in your verses by putting them on the balancing line (usually the fourth or final line) of each verse?

—Have you made key phrases more impactful and memorable by placing them on a balancing line that ends with an unexpected imperfect rhyme?

—Have you included an occasional surprising rhyme or intriguing phrase that can attract listeners' attention and make them stop and think?

—Have you used the bridge (or 'middle eight') to advance the story by building on the lyrical drama created in the verses and chorus?

—Does your bridge add crucial new information to the storyline—perhaps delivering an unexpected twist or a new revelation?

—Have you made sure the song's title doesn't appear in the bridge, so listeners won't think it's just another chorus?

—Have you avoided an imbalance in your lyrics by making sure corresponding lyric lines in the verses are the same length (with the same number of syllables) in every verse?

—Have you avoided an imbalance by making sure corresponding lyric lines in the chorus are the same length (with the same number of syllables) in every repeated chorus?

—Have you included enough lyrical contrast to make each section of the song sound different from the other segments?

—Have you built plenty of variation into your metric structure (including different line lengths and different rhythmic patterns) to establish a clear distinction between your verses, chorus and bridge?

—Have you matched the rhythmic sound patterns of syllables within each line to the patterns imposed by the beats and tempo of the music?

—Have you given your chorus a meter that has shorter lyric lines than the verses so it is more direct and memorable?

—Are you sure listeners will be able to tell where the verse ends and the chorus begins?

—Have you made sure your lyrics in the verses mostly use descriptive words, while the chorus and bridge lyrics express emotions?

—Do your verse lyrics build the tension and move the song forward in a logical sequence so that each verse is like a new chapter in a book?

—Have you used the active voice rather than the passive voice?

—Have you tried to tell the story from a different or unexpected perspective?

—Have you avoided using phrases, descriptions, rhymes and metaphors that you've used before in your other lyrics?

—When developing your lyrics, did you ask yourself the What, Why, When, How, Where and Who questions?

—Are you sure you've given listeners enough detail to help them see the mental images, and feel the emotions, that you wanted to convey?

—Have you *shown* listeners what's happening in your story instead of just telling them?

—Do your lyrics paint a picture rather than simply convey information?

—Have you painted vivid word pictures that describe the physical experience of the emotions that you want to convey?

—Have you described each scene as if you're looking through a video camera, so listeners can 'see' and experience what the singer's feeling?

—Have you used 'show' devices such as personification, similes and metaphors?

—Have you tried to avoid using clichés so that your lyrics don't sound boring and predictable?

—Have you used some original rhymes, or tried a new twist on an old theme, to make your lyrics sound fresh and inventive?

—Have you checked to make sure you haven't used the same rhyme sound too many times in a row in your verses, so your rhymes won't be too predictable?

—Have you made sure the rhyme scheme chosen for the verse is the same in every verse (even though the words are different)?

—Have you varied the rhyme schemes in the verse, chorus and bridge so that each section sounds different and has its own personality?

—Does your rhyme scheme in the verses and pre-chorus (if you have one) build urgency and momentum to prepare listeners for the all-important hook in the chorus?

—Are you using lyrical images and descriptive phrases that are easily understood and can connect with the listener?

—Have you worked on developing your sensory writing skills?

—Have you used the five physical senses to enrich your word pictures and help bring your lyrics to life?

—Have you used strong, descriptive verbs, so you didn't have to rely too much on adjectives and adverbs?

—Have you used active verbs to convey action, drama, conflict and motion?

—Have you kept your imagery simple, using everyday words imaginatively to create realistic images?

—Have you checked the 'singability' of your lyrics so that artists will be able to sing your words comfortably?

—Have you checked every word, phrase and syllable to make sure they sing effortlessly?

—Have you built in rests and pauses so that the singer has space to breathe?

—Have you made sure you haven't included any unintentional 'tongue twisters'?

—Have you checked to make sure you haven't used any adjoining words that, when sung, could be misheard and misunderstood by listeners?

—Have you gone through a comprehensive editing and re-writing process to make sure your lyrics are as strong as possible?

—Are you confident that the song is strong enough for you to spend time and money on it at the demo stage?

—Are you sure you have the final version of the lyrics so you won't have to spend time making further changes in the studio at the demo stage?

—Have you made sure the vocal and lyrics are crystal clear on your demo of the song, with the lead vocal upfront in the mix?

—Have you mixed your demo down to small speakers or headphones to make sure publishers, A&R execs and producers will hear your words clearly at that sound level?

—Have you tested your lyrics and your demo on someone who will give you an honest opinion before you go ahead and submit the song?

# # # #

IF YOU'VE ticked most of the boxes in this comprehensive checklist, then it looks like you're in good shape.

I hope this book has been useful to you in highlighting the key components that are consistently found in the lyrical structure of all hit songs.

And I hope it will help you to avoid the most common errors that are often made when these various elements are built into a song.

Best wishes for great success with your songs and your lyrics. And always remember this advice from Diane Warren, one of the most successful female songwriters of all time:

"You've got to believe ... Believe in yourself. Believe in your work."

# # # #

Other books by Brian Oliver

"HOW [NOT] TO WRITE A HIT SONG!"

101 COMMON MISTAKES TO AVOID IF YOU WANT SONGWRITING SUCCESS

Written in an easy, non-technical style, this book takes a close look at the essential elements consistently found in the structure, melodies and lyrics of all hit songs. It highlights the most common errors made when these key components are built into a song—so that new songwriters can try to avoid such mistakes in their own songs.

# # # #

Five-star praise for "HOW [NOT] TO WRITE A HIT SONG!" from verified purchasers*:

"The best book on song writing that I have ever read. I've been writing songs for 15 years and I was worried that I would know most of it already, but I learnt a lot of new things and it has definitely improved my song writing. It is good for both beginners and experienced song writers. I wish I had read this book when I first started out as it would have saved me a lot of time that I wasted on trial and error."

—Heather

"The best songwriting book ever. This is an absolutely brilliant book for the aspiring or established songwriter. I am very impressed. It is concise, easy to read and on point. A must read if you are aiming to write a HIT song!"

—Y. Vernon

"This book is just superb. I am quite new to song writing but this book has helped me immeasurably. It explains every step of the process. Really is a great motivator to get them down on paper and through to recording. Don't miss this book. I've looked at a few but this for me was easily the best."

—Jan Zienkiewicz

"Fantastic book. Well written, great advice for the hopeful songwriter. Spot on."

—Mark Edward Purvis

"This book is a must for the aspiring songwriter. As well as detailed information about the pitfalls of a newcomer to the market, the book also highlights the tried and tested successful Verse-Chorus-Verse progressions etc. Being new to song writing myself, I revisited some old songs after reading this book and reworked them using some of the advice given and I have to say they are greatly improved...Well worth buying even if you think you have mastered the art... Recommended."

—G.T.

"A fantastically useful book. This is a book that does exactly what it says on the cover, and it does it in an entertaining and practical way. No words are wasted, there isn't a rambling preface or lengthy introduction, it just gets stuck in straight away."
 —'A fingerstyle guitarist'

"Excellent book."
 —Ron

*All verified Amazon purchasers

# # # #

Printed in Great Britain
by Amazon